Cr ... ing

AND OTHER NEEDLEWORK CRAFTS

including

TENERIFFE LACE
KNITTED LACE
NETTING
HAIRPIN LACE CROCHET
BRAIDWORK FRINGES TASSELS

EDITED BY

Helen Crosier

★ CONTENTS ★

☆ CROCHET ☆

First Steps

So you've never crocheted before? Well, here's where you start learning how easy it is. Follow the steps on the next three pages—or if you are left-handed, on pages 9 to 11—and there, practically before you can say *Jack Robinson,* you've got all the hand positions at your finger tips and can even make a chain. From there on it's easy to learn the other stitches and make all the pretty things in this book.

Practice Pieces

Directions are given for a small practice piece or swatch for each stitch that you learn. When you have learned these stitches you can start on the articles which can be made from the directions given in this book.

Crochet Hooks

Crochet hooks are made of steel, composition or bone. Steel crochet hooks range in size from number 2/0, the largest, to number 7, the smallest. Composition or bone hooks range in sizes from number 6, the largest, to number 12, the smallest. Each is especially adapted for use with a certain size of thread. To ensure the correct results, it is important that you use the number hook specified in the directions.

Crochet Threads

Remember that texture plays an important part in the beauty of crochet. The finer mercerised threads are more effective for the delicate designs used for tablecloths, doilies, edgings and accessories.

If you work with your RIGHT hand

STEP 1. MAKE A LOOP

1. Grasp thread near end between thumb and forefinger of left hand.
2. With right hand make a loop by lapping long thread over short thread.
3. Hold loop in place between thumb and forefinger of left hand (Fig. 1).

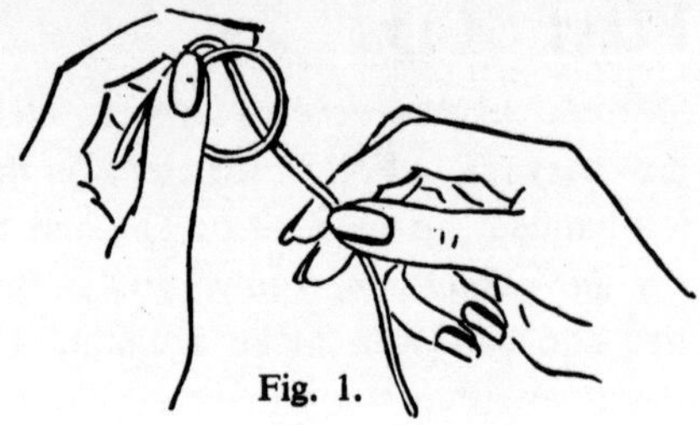

Fig. 1.

STEP 2

1. With right hand take hold of broad bar of hook as you would a pencil.
2. Insert hook through loop and under long thread. With right hand catch long end of thread (Fig. 2). Draw loop through.
3. Do not remove hook from thread.

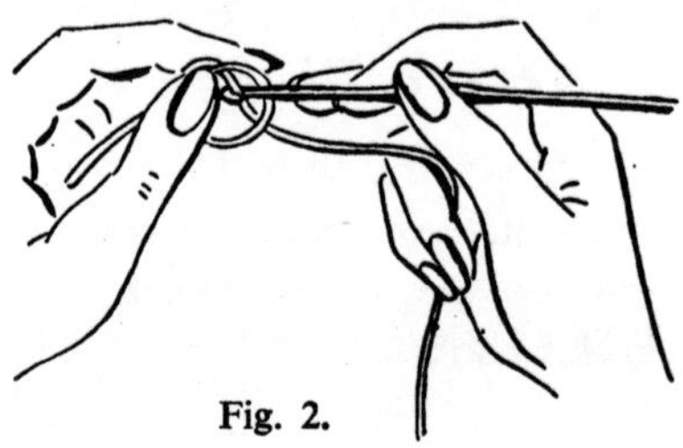

Fig. 2.

STEP 3

1. Pull short end and ball thread in opposite directions to bring loop close around the end of the hook, but not too tight (Fig. 3).

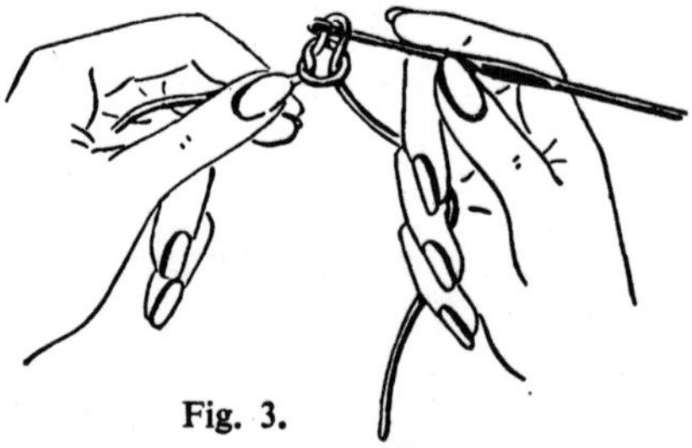

Fig. 3.

STEP 4. WHAT TO DO WITH THE LEFT HAND

1. Measure with your eye about 4 inches along ball thread from loop on hook.
2. At about this point insert thread between ring and little fingers, having palm of hand facing up (Fig. 4).

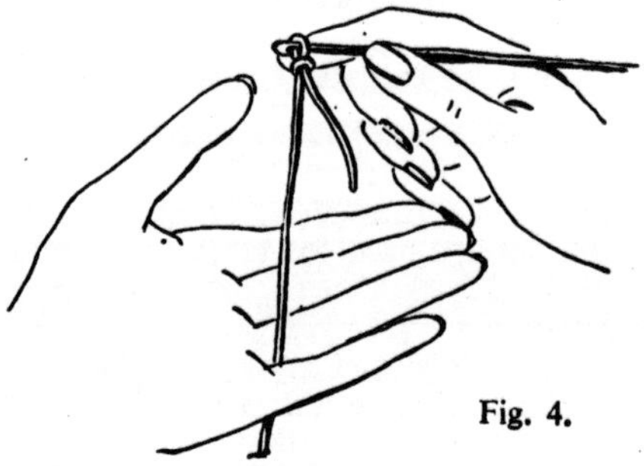

Fig. 4.

If you work with your RIGHT hand

STEP 5

1. Bring thread toward back, under little and ring fingers, over middle finger, and under the forefinger toward the thumb (Fig. 5).

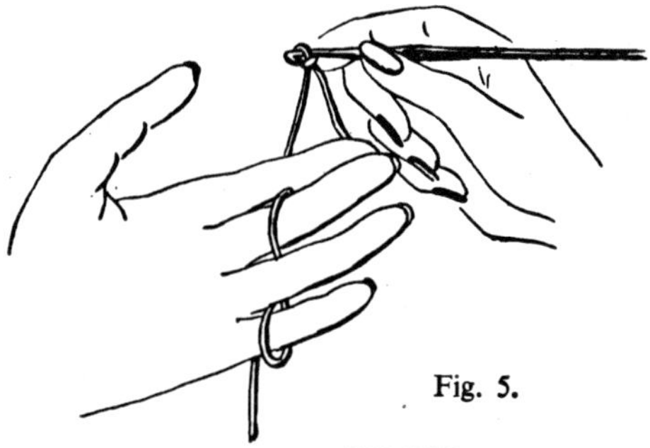

Fig. 5.

STEP 6

1. Grasp hook and loop between thumb and forefinger of left hand.

2. Gently pull ball thread so that it lies around the fingers firmly but not tightly (Fig. 6).

3. Catch knot of loop between thumb and forefinger.

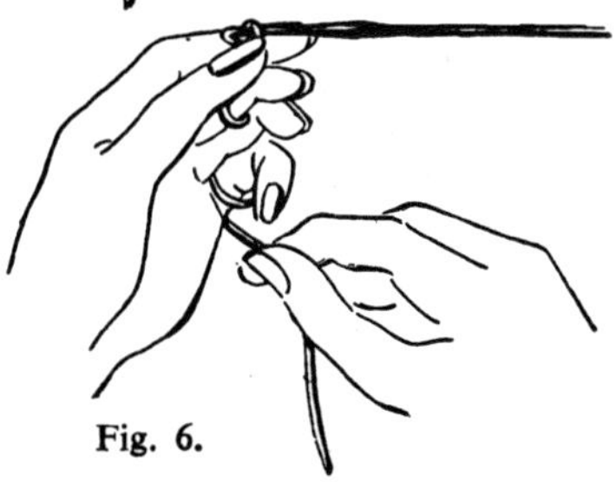

Fig. 6.

STEP 7. WHAT TO DO WITH THE RIGHT HAND

1. Take hold of broad bar of hook as you would a pencil.

2. Bring middle finger forward to rest near tip of hook (Fig. 7).

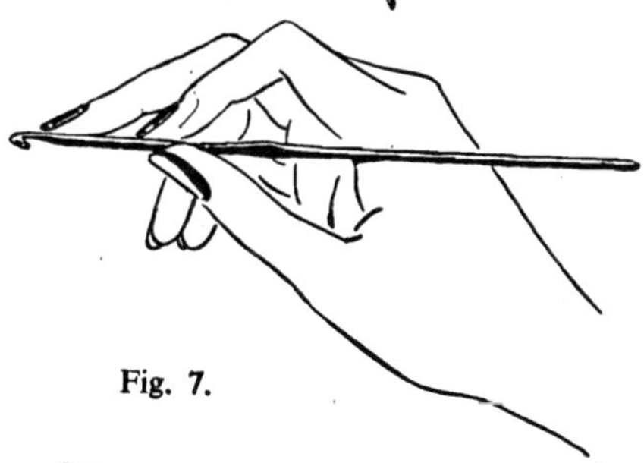

Fig. 7.

STEP 8. CHAIN STITCH
Abbreviation—ch

1. Adjust fingers of left hand as in Fig. 8—the middle finger is bent to regulate the tension, the ring and little fingers control the thread. The *motion* of the *hook* in the *right hand* and the *thread* in the *left hand* should be free and even. Ease comes with practice.

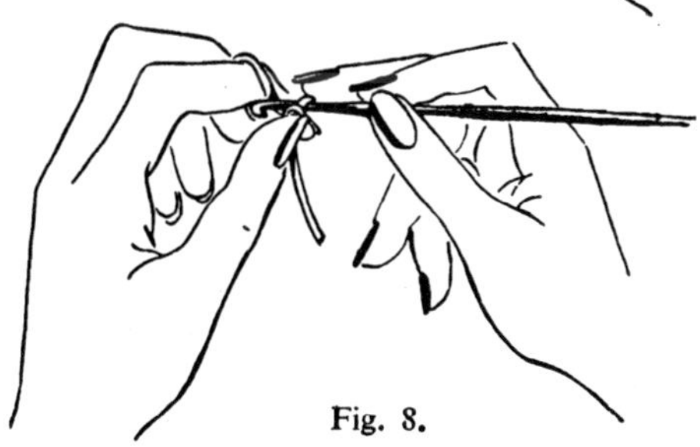

Fig. 8.

If you work with your RIGHT hand

STEP 9

1. Pass your hook under thread and catch thread with hook. This is called 'thread over' (Fig. 9).

2. Draw thread through loop on hook. This makes one chain (ch).

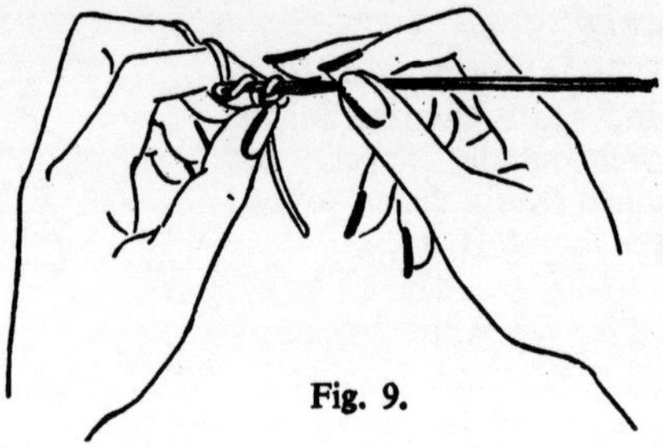

Fig. 9.

STEP 10

1. Repeat Step 9 until you have as many chain stitches (ch sts) as you need—1 loop always remains on the hook (Fig. 10).

2. Always keep thumb and forefinger of left hand near stitch on which you are working.

3. Practise making chain stitches until they are even in size.

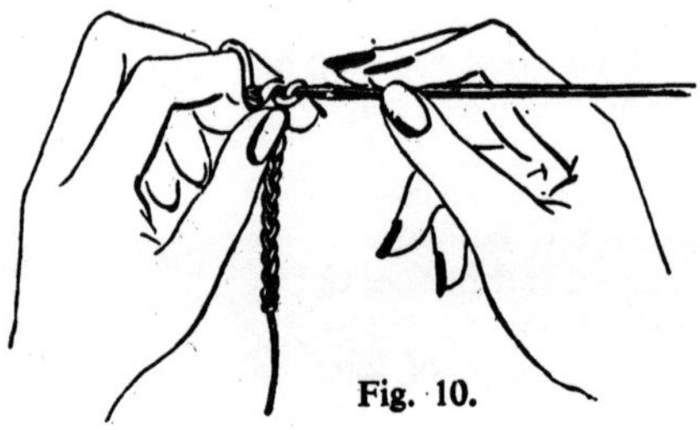

Fig. 10.

If you work with your LEFT hand

All left-handers can say hurray: Here is one book of crochet instructions that has not forgotten you. You follow the ten steps on the following pages. Next you study very carefully the warning marked STOP! LOOK! LISTEN! (page 11), and from then on it will be smooth sailing and happy crocheting!

STEP 1. MAKE A LOOP

1. Grasp thread near end between thumb and forefinger of right hand.
2. With left hand make a loop by lapping long thread over short thread.
3. Hold loop in place between thumb and forefinger of right hand (Fig. 1).

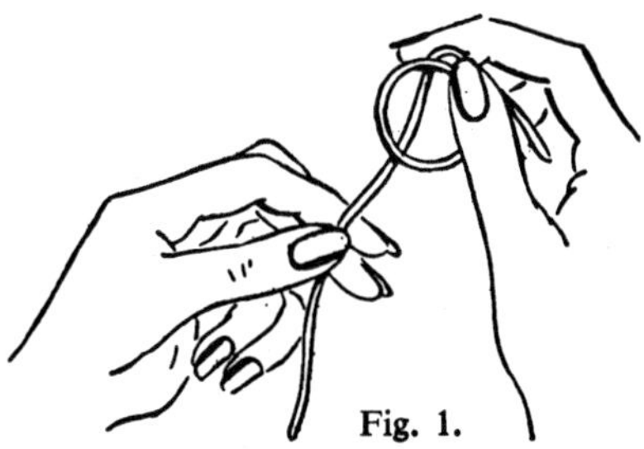

Fig. 1.

STEP 2

1. With left hand take hold of broad bar of hook as you would a pencil.
2. Insert hook through loop and under long thread. With left hand catch long end of thread (Fig. 2). Draw loop through.
3. Do not remove hook from thread.

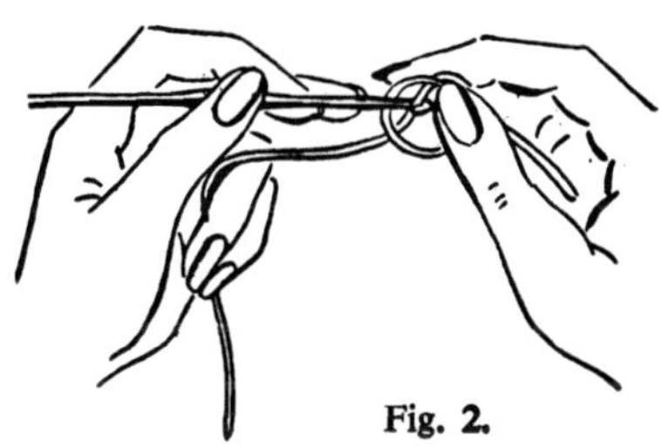

Fig. 2.

STEP 3

1. Pull short end and ball thread in opposite directions to bring loop close around the end of the hook, but not too tight (Fig. 3).

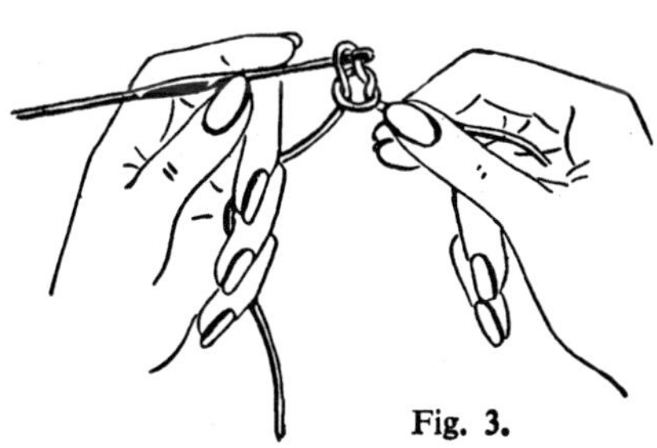

Fig. 3.

If you work with your LEFT hand

STEP 4. WHAT TO DO WITH THE RIGHT HAND

1. Measure with your eye about 4 inches along ball thread from loop on hook.
2. At about this point insert thread between your ring and little fingers, having palm of hand facing up (Fig. 4).

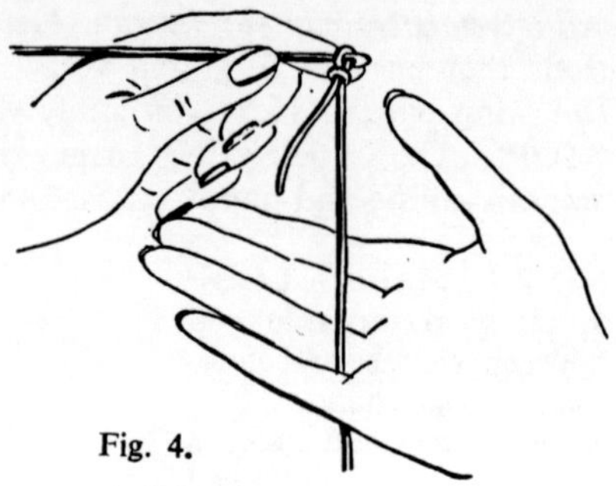

Fig. 4.

STEP 5

1. Bring thread toward back, under little and ring fingers, over the middle finger, and under the forefinger toward the thumb (Fig. 5).

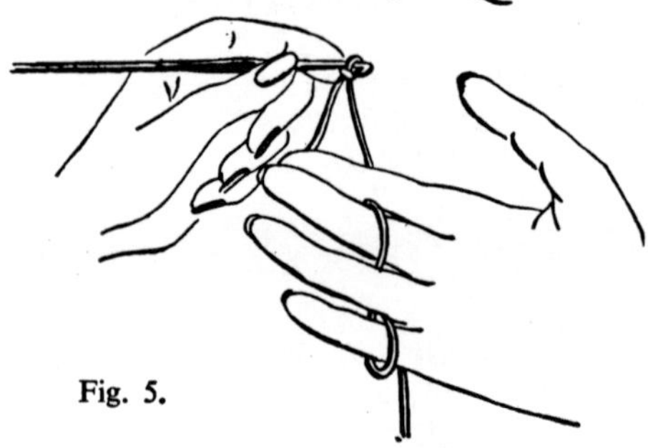

Fig. 5.

STEP 6

1. Grasp hook and loop between thumb and forefinger of right hand.
2. Gently pull ball thread so that it lies around the fingers firmly but not tightly (Fig. 6).
3. Catch knot of loop between thumb and forefinger.

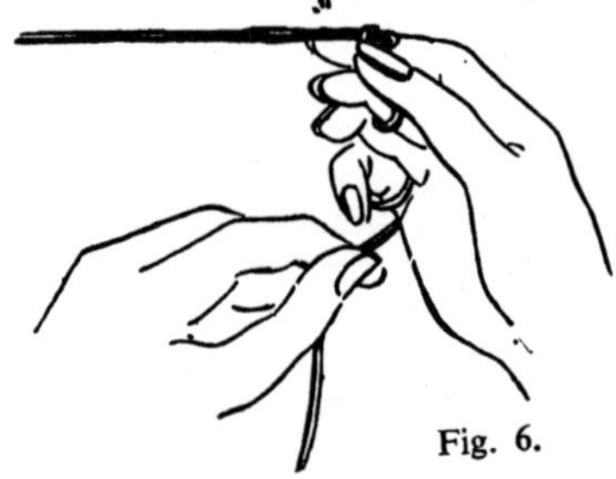

Fig. 6.

STEP 7. WHAT TO DO WITH THE LEFT HAND

1. Take hold of broad bar of hook as you would a pencil.
2. Bring middle finger forward to rest near tip of hook (Fig. 7).

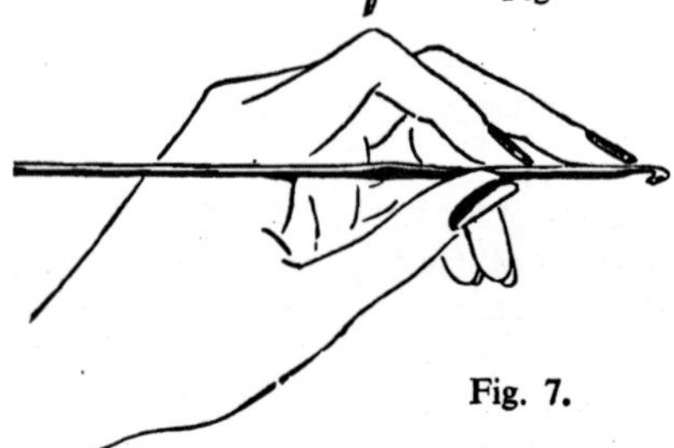

Fig. 7.

If you work with your LEFT hand

STEP 8. CHAIN STITCH

Abbreviation—ch

1. Adjust fingers of right hand as in Fig. 8—the middle finger is bent to regulate the tension, the ring and little fingers control the thread. The *motion* of the *hook* in the *left hand* and the *thread* in the *right hand* should be free and even. Ease comes with practice.

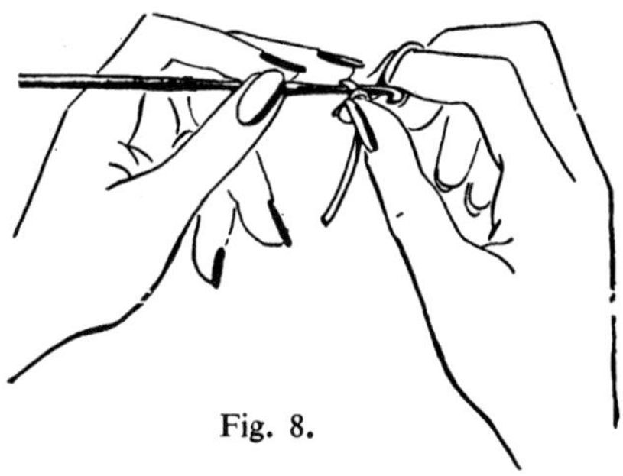

Fig. 8.

STEP 9

1. Pass your hook under thread and catch thread with hook. This is called 'thread over' (Fig. 9).

2. Draw thread through loop on hook. This makes one chain (ch).

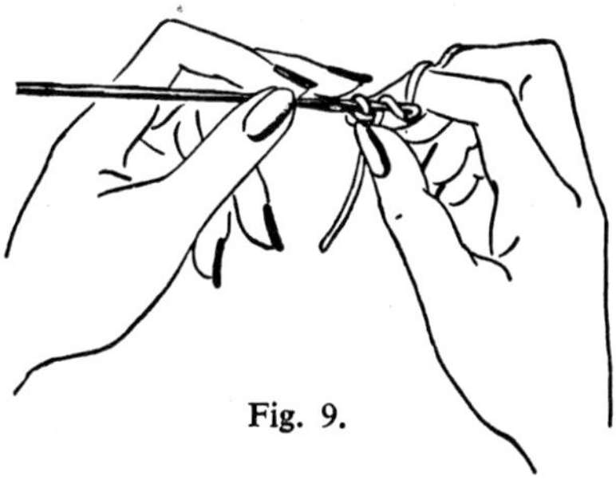

Fig. 9.

STEP 10

1. Repeat Step 9 until you have as many chain stitches (ch sts) as you need—1 loop always remains on the hook (Fig. 10).

2. Always keep thumb and forefinger of your right hand near stitch on which you are working.

3. Practise making chain stitches until they are even in size.

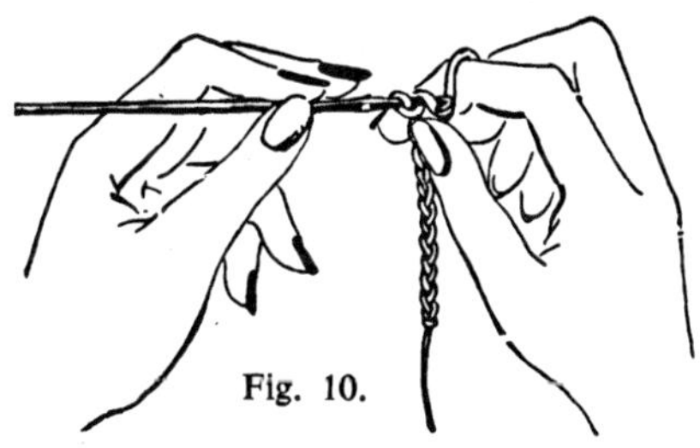

Fig. 10.

LEFT-HANDERS: STOP! LOOK! AND LISTEN!

All illustrations of stitches shown on the following pages are in position for the **Right-handed** pupil.

Right-handed pupils work from **Right to Left. Left-handed** pupils work from **Left to Right.** The directions for each stitch apply to both **Right- and Left-handed** pupils.

For Left-handed Pupils Only: Place a pocket mirror to the left of each illustration and you will see the exact position in which you work reflected in the mirror.

Crochet Abbreviations

ch	chain
ss	slip stitch
dc	double crochet
hlf tr	half treble
tr	treble
dbl tr	double treble
trip tr	triple treble
quad tr	quadruple treble
rnd	round
blk	block
sp	space
st(s)	stitch(es)

* (asterisk) . . . repeat the instructions following the asterisk as many more times as specified, in addition to the original.

Repeat instructions in parentheses as many times as specified. For example: '(5 ch, dc in next dc) 5 times' means to make all in parentheses 5 times in all.

HOW TO TURN AT END OF ROW

Double Crochet (dc)	1 ch to turn
Half Treble (hlf tr)	2 ch to turn
Treble (tr)	3 ch to turn
Double Treble (dbl tr)	4 ch to turn
Triple Treble (trip tr)	5 ch to turn
Quadruple Treble (quad tr)	6 ch to turn

Note. In all crochet it is customary to pick up the 2 top loops (or threads) of each stitch as you work, unless otherwise specified.

Rows of Double Crochet

(Abbreviation—dc)

Making a starting chain of 20 stitches for a practice piece.

FIRST ROW (1st row)

STEP 1. Insert hook from the front under the 2 top threads of 2nd ch from hook (Fig. 11).

Fig. 11

STEP 2. Catch thread with hook—this is known as 'thread over' (Fig. 12).

Fig. 12.

STEP 3. Draw thread through chain. There are 2 loops on hook (Fig. 13).

Fig. 13.

STEP 4. Thread over (Fig. 14) and draw through 2 loops—1 loop remains on hook.

Fig. 14.

STEP 5. You have now completed 1 double crotchet (dc) (Fig. 15).

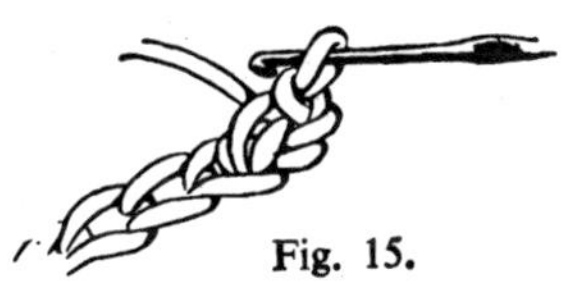

Fig. 15.

STEP 6. For next double crochet (dc), insert hook under 2 top threads of next ch and repeat Steps 2 to 6.

STEP 7. Repeat Step 6 until you have made a double crochet (dc) in each ch.

STEP 8. At end of row of double crochets, 1 ch (Fig. 16). The 1 ch enables you to turn your work more easily.

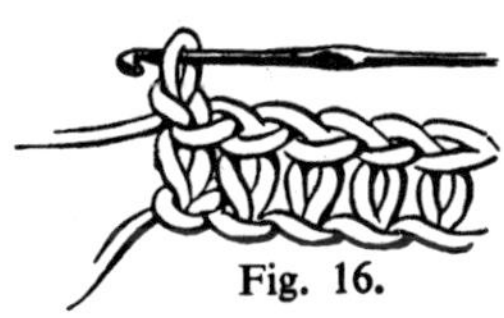

Fig. 16.

STEP 9. Turn your work so that the reverse side is facing you (Fig. 17).

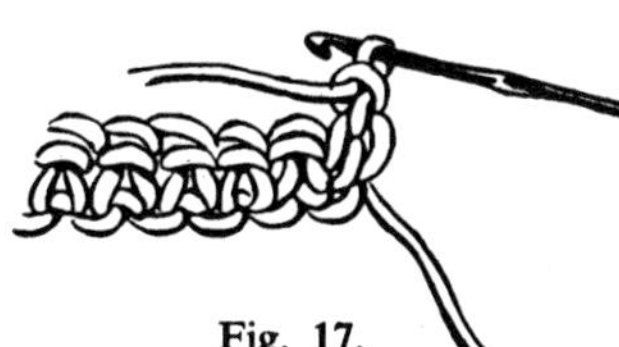

Fig. 17.

Rows of Double Crochet
(continued)

SECOND ROW (2nd row)

STEP 1. Insert hook from the front under the 2 top loops of first stitch (st)—the last stitch made on previous row.

STEP 2. Catch thread with hook ('thread over') and draw through st —2 loops remain on hook.

STEP 3. Thread over and draw through 2 loops—1 loop remains on hook.

STEP 4. For next double crochet (dc), insert hook from the front under the 2 top loops of next st and repeat Steps 2 and 3.

STEP 5. Repeat Steps 4, 2 and 3 until you have made a double crochet (dc) in each st. 1 ch and turn.

STEP 6. Repeat Second Row until you are familiar with this stitch. Break off (Fig. 18).

HOW TO 'BREAK OFF'

STEP 1. Do not make a turning chain at end of last row.

STEP 2. Clip thread about 3 inches from work, bring loose end through the one remaining loop on hook and pull tightly (Fig. 18).

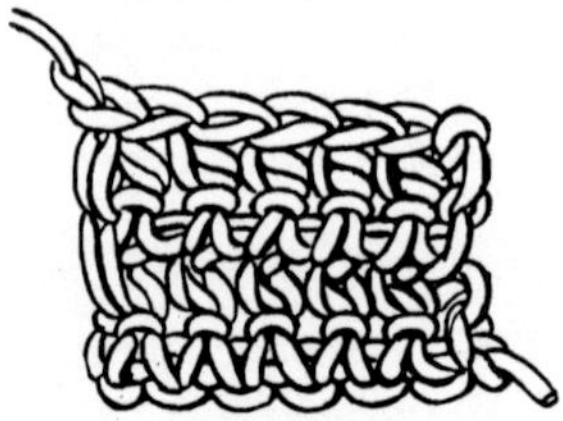

Fig. 18

HOW TO TURN YOUR WORK

In crochet a certain number of chain stitches are added at the end of each row to bring work in position for the next row. Then the work is turned so that the reverse side is facing the worker. You have noticed that in double crochet 1 ch only is used for turning. The number of turning chains depends upon the stitch with which you intend to begin the next row. Listed on page 12 are the **turning chains** for each of the basic stitches.

›ouble Crochet ;vening Belt

ee overleaf)

n't this a lovely way to ›ok at night? All you ›ed is any simple dark ›ess. Just watch the ay it lights up with this ›on white belt glittering ith pearls and tiny gold ›quins. There's a tiny ›uare pocket for lipstick ›d hankie.

Double Crochet Evening Belt

(*See previous page*)

Materials. Mercer-Crochet No. 40 (20 gram). 4 balls selected colour. 4 buttons. Milwards' Steel Crochet Hook No. 3.

Use 2 threads throughout (1 thread from each of 2 balls).

This belt is begun at one long side.

Directions. To begin, make a chain 2 inches longer than waist measurement.

1st Row. Dc (double crochet) in 2nd (second) ch (chain) from hook, 1 dc into each ch across, 1 ch, turn.

2nd and 3rd rows. 1 dc (double crochet) into each dc across, 1 ch, turn.

4th row. 1 dc (double crochet) into each dc across to last 9 dc, 6 ch (chain), miss 6 dc, 1 dc into each of last 3 dc (the 6 ch forms a button-hole), 1 ch, turn.

5th row. 1 dc into each of next 3 dc, 6 dc over next 6 ch, 1 dc into each dc, 1 ch, turn.

6th to 13th row. Repeat 2nd to 5th row twice.

14th and 15th rows. Repeat 2nd and 3rd rows. Break off at end of 15th row. Sew on buttons to correspond with button holes.

POCKET

1st row. Commence with 21 ch and work as for first row of belt (20 dc on row), 1 ch, turn.

2nd row. As 2nd row of belt, 1 ch, turn. Repeat 2nd row until piece measures 6½ inches from beginning.

Next Row. 1 dc into each of next 7 dc, 6 ch, miss 6 dc, 1 dc into each of next 7 dc (button-hole), 1 ch, turn.

Last Row. 1 dc into each of next 7 dc, 6 dc over 6 ch, 1 dc into each of next 7 dc. Break off. Fold the beginning of pocket back to measure 2½ inches. Sew up sides. Fold remainder of pocket over to form a flap. Sew on button to correspond with button-hole. Sew pocket to belt. Trim belt and pocket with sequins and beads.

How to follow the Asterisk (*)

Sometimes in the directions you will see the following phrases:

1. Repeat from * across.
2. Repeat from * all round.
3. Repeat from * 3 (or any number) more times.

In Nos. 1 and 2 follow the directions from the first to the last * (asterisk) completely across row or all round. In No. 3 follow the directions from the first * (asterisk) as many times as specified.

Rounds of Double Crochet

STEP 1. Make a chain (ch) of 4 stitches (sts). Join with slip stitch (ss) in 1st ch to form a ring (Figs. 19 and 20).

Fig. 19.

STEP 2. 1st rnd (round). Make 8 double crochet (dc) in ring (Fig. 21). **Place a safety pin in the last dc of 1st rnd to mark end of rnd. Move the safety pin to the last dc of the following rnds.**

Fig. 20.

STEP 3. 2nd rnd. 2 double crochet (dc) in each dc of previous rnd. There are 16 dc on rnd (Fig. 22).

STEP 4. 3rd rnd. * 2 double crochet (dc) in next dc—an increase made in last dc (Fig. 22), dc in next dc. Repeat from * all round (24 dc on rnd).

Fig. 21.

STEP 5. 4th rnd. * Double crochet (dc) in next 2 dc, 2 dc in next **dc** (increase made in last dc). Repeat from * all round (32 dc on rnd).

STEP 6. 5th rnd. * Double crochet (dc) in next 3 dc, 2 dc in next dc. Repeat from * all round (40 dc on rnd).

STEP 7. 6th rnd. Double crochet (dc) in each dc all round. Slip stitch (ss) in next 2 **dc** (Figs. 19 and 20). Break off (Fig. 18).

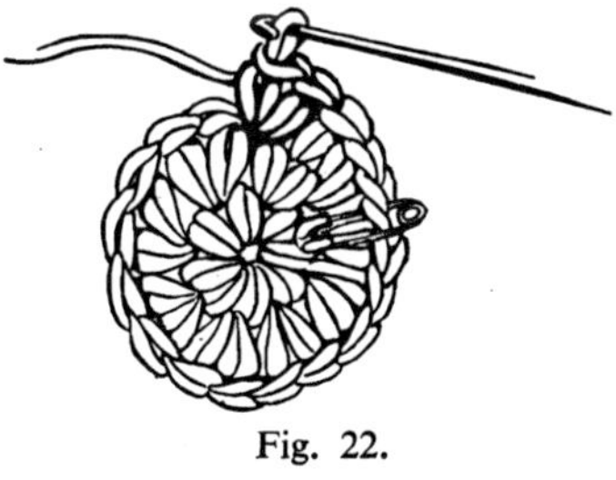

Fig. 22.

SLIP STITCH—Abbreviation—ss

It is not necessary to make a practice piece for slip stitch (ss) because it is seldom used except when an invisible stitch is required. When the directions say **join,** you always use a slip stitch.

STEP 1. Insert hook from the front through the 2 top threads of chain (Fig. 19).

STEP 2. Thread over and with one motion draw through chain and loop on hook—1 loop remains on hook (Fig. 20). This completes a slip stitch (ss).

Double Crochet Shoulder Bag and Hat

Materials. Mercer-Crochet No. 40 (20 gram.). 6 balls selected colour for Hat. 9 balls selected colour for Bag. 3 Wooden Button Moulds. Buckram and Lining to match for Bag. 1 Press Stud. Milwards' Steel Crochet Hook No. 2½. (Slack workers could use a No. 3 hook and tight workers a No. 2.)

Tension. 9 rows=2 in. in diameter.

Abbreviations. ch—chain; ss—slip-stitch; dc—double crochet; st—stitch.

Use three thicknesses of thread throughout.

BAG.

Front. Commence with 8 ch, join with ss to form a ring.

1st Row. Into ring work 12 dc.

2nd Row. 2 dc into each dc.

Continue working rows of dc increasing sufficient to keep work flat until work measures 9 in. in diameter, ending with 1 ss into first dc. Fasten off.

Back. Work as for front.

Gusset. Work a chain 26 in. long.

1st Row. 3 dc into 2nd ch from hook, 1 dc into each ch, 3 dc into last ch, work down other side of ch to correspond.

2nd Row. 1 dc into each dc, working 3 dc into centre dc at each point. Repeat 2nd row 8 times more, ending with 1 ss into first dc. Fasten off.

Shoulder Strap. Work a chain 30 in. long. Work same as gusset.

Fastening Strap. Work a chain 6 in. long. Work first 2 rows as for gusset.

Fastening Button. Work a chain 2 in. long. Work first 4 rows as for gusset. Cover button moulds with rows of dc.

To Make-Up

Line front and back pieces with buckram and then lining. Line gusset and shoulder strap also with buckram and lining. Sew back and front to gusset leaving 2½ in. free at each point of gusset. Sew each point of shoulder strap under points of gusset. Sew covered moulds at centre of back and front. Fold fastening strap length-wise and over-cast last row together, then sew at top of back (at opening). Cover a small piece of wood with lining and over-cast small piece of crochet to this, thus forming fastening button. Sew to front of bag at centre top. Sew on press stud.

DOUBLE CROCHET SHOULDER BAG AND HAT

CROCHET * page 20

HAT CROWN

Commence with 4 ch, join with ss to form a ring.

1st Row. Into ring work 6 dc.

2nd Row. 2 dc into each dc.

Continue working rows of dc increasing sufficient to keep work flat, until work measures $8\frac{3}{4}$ in. in diameter having 255 dc on last row, 1 ss into first dc, fasten off.

Under Part

Commence with 181 ch, join with ss to form a ring.

1st Row. 1 dc into each ch (180 dc).

2nd Row. I dc into each dc.

Repeat 2nd row 5 times more. Place a marking thread to indicate end of row, centre back.

8th Row. Increase 36 dc having an equal distance between each increase, fasten off.

9th Row. Miss 89 dc, join thread on next dc, 1 dc into each of the next 36 dc, 1 ss into next dc, fasten off. **10th Row.** Join thread at centre back and work 1 row of dc having 1 dc into same place where thread was joined and 1 dc into same place as ss, fasten off. **11th Row.** Miss 83 dc, join thread on next dc, 1 dc into each of next 42 dc, 1 ss into next dc, fasten off. **12th Row.** As 10th row. **13th Row.** As 11th row, joining thread 6 dc nearer centre back and finishing 6 dc nearer centre back (12 dc more at front). **14th Row.** As 10th row increasing 27 dc and varying position of increases. **15th Row.** As 11th row. Repeat 10th and 11th rows twice more. **20th Row.** As 10th row increasing 12 dc varying position of increases (255 dc). **21st Row.** As 11th row. Repeat 10th and 11th rows twice more. **26th Row.** As 10th row.

Band

Join thread at centre back of foundation ch and work 8 rows of dc (180 dc).

Next Row. 1 ss into each dc, fasten off.

Bow

Commence with 2 ch.

1st Row. 3 dc into 2nd ch from hook, 1 ch, turn.

2nd Row. Increase 1 st at beginning of row, 1 ch, turn. Repeat 2nd row until there are 12 dc.

Next Row. I dc into each dc, 1 ch, turn.

Repeat last row 97 times more.

Next Row. Decrease 1 st at beginning of next row, 1 ch, turn. (To decrease—insert hook into first dc and pull loop through, insert hook into next dc and pull loop through, thread over and pull through all loops on hook.)

Repeat last row until 3 sts remain. Decrease 2 sts, fasten off.

Band for Bow

Commence with 19 ch.

1st Row. 1 dc into 2nd ch from hook, 1 dc into each ch, 1 ch, turn.

2nd Row. 1 dc into each dc, 1 ch, turn. Repeat 2nd row twice more, fasten off.

Button Mould

Cover button mould with rows of dc.

To Make-Up

Join crown and under part by overcasting the two edges together. Make up bow and sew at side front. Sew button mould to centre of crown.

Rows of Half Treble Crochet

(Abbreviation—hlf tr)

Making a starting chain of 20 stitches for practice piece.

Notice when working rounds of hlf tr that there is an extra loop on the wrong side directly below the 2 top loops of each hlf tr. **Work only in the 2 top loops of each stitch.**

FIRST ROW (1st row)

STEP 1. Pass hook under the thread of left hand (this is called 'thread over'—Fig. 23).

STEP 2. Insert hook from the front under the 2 top loops (or threads) of 3rd ch from hook.

STEP 3. Thread over hook and pull loop through chain (3 loops on hook), thread over (Fig. 24).

STEP 4. Draw through all loops on hook—1 loop remains on hook (Fig. 25). A half treble (hlf tr) is now completed.

STEP 5. For next half treble (hlf tr), thread over, insert hook from front under the 2 top threads of next ch.

STEP 6. Repeat Steps 3, 4 and 5 until you have made a hlf tr in each ch.

STEP 7. At end of row, ch 2 (Fig. 26) and turn.

SECOND ROW (2nd row)

STEP 1. Thread over hook, insert hook from front under the 2 top loops of first stitch (st)—the last st on previous row.

STEP 2. Thread over hook and pull through stitch—there are 3 loops on hook; thread over and draw through all loops on hook.

STEP 3. For next half treble (hlf tr), thread over hook, insert hook from the front under the 2 top loops of next stitch (st) and repeat Step 2.

STEP 4. Repeat Steps 3 and 2 until you have made a half treble (hlf tr) in each stitch, (st), 2 ch and turn.

STEP 5. The turning 2 ch of each row does not count as a stitch on the following row.

STEP 6. Repeat Second Row (2nd row) until you are familiar with this stitch. Break off at end of last row (Fig. 18).

Fig. 23.

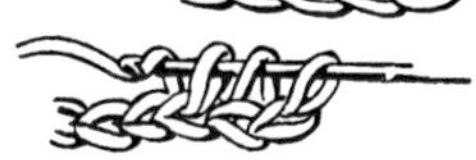

Fig. 24

Fig. 25.

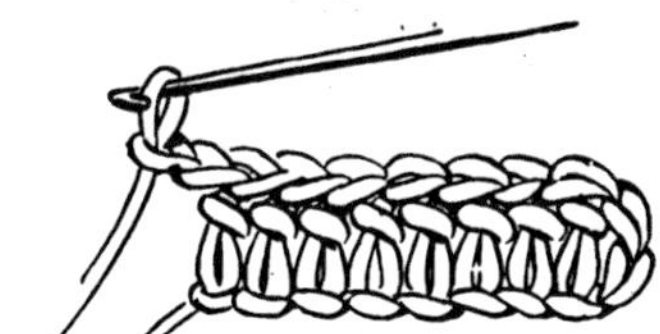

Fig. 26.

HALF TREBLE CROCHET VANITY CASE

Materials. Mercer-Crochet No. 40 (20 gram). 2 balls selected colour. Milwards' Steel Crochet Hook No. 4. Commence at top edge, make a chain 8 in. long (13 sts to 1 in.).

1st Row. 1 hlf tr into 3rd ch from hook, 1 hlf tr into each ch across until row measures 6 in. Cut off remaining chain, 2 ch, turn.

2nd Row. Miss first tr, 1 hlf tr into each hlf tr across, 2 ch, turn. Repeat 2nd row until piece measures 12 in., 2 ch, turn.

FLAP

Decrease 1 hlf tr at both ends of every other row until 26 sts remain—to decrease, work off 2 hlf tr as for 1 hlf tr. To work off 2 hlf tr as 1 hlf tr, * thread over, draw a loop through next hlf tr; repeat from * once more (5 loops on hook—Fig. 27), thread over and draw through all loops on hook (Fig. 28).
Break off.

RUFFLE

1st Row. Attach thread to last straight row and work dc closely along curved edge of flap, 5 ch, turn.

2nd Row. * 1 dc into next dc, 5 ch; repeat from * across, 7 ch, turn.

3rd, 4th and 5th Rows. * 1 dc into next loop, 5 ch; repeat from * across, 7 ch, turn. Omit turning chain at end of 5th row. Break off. Fold straight piece in half and sew up sides. Line and fasten with a press stud.

Rounds of Half Treble Crochet

Notice there is an extra loop directly below the 2 top loops of each hlf tr. **Work only in the 2 top loops.**

STEP 1. Make a chain of 4 stitches (sts). Join with slip stitch (ss) in 1st ch to form a ring (Figs. 19 and 20).

STEP 2. 1st rnd. 2 ch, 11 half treble crochet (hlf tr) in ring (Fig. 29).

STEP 3. Place a safety-pin in the last hlf tr of 1st rnd to mark end of rnd. Move the safety-pin to the last hlf tr of the following rnds.

STEP 4. 2nd rnd. 2 half treble (hlf tr) in each hlf tr all round (22 hlf tr on round).

STEP 5. 3rd rnd. Half treble (hlf tr) in each hlf tr all round (22 hlf tr on round).

STEP 6. 4th rnd. * Half treble (hlf tr) in next hlf tr, 2 hlf tr in next hlf tr. Repeat from * all round (Fig. 30)—33 hlf tr on rnd.

STEP 7. 5th rnd. Half treble (hlf tr) in each hlf tr all round.

STEP 8. 6th rnd. 2 half treble (hlf tr) in each hlf tr all round (66 hlf tr on rnd).

STEP 9. 7th rnd. Half treble (hlf tr) in each hlf tr all round. Ss in next 2 hlf tr (Figs. 19 and 20). Break off (Fig. 18).

STEP 10. If a larger circle is desired, **do not break off** but increase 9 hlf tr evenly on each rnd to keep work flat. Do not have increases fall over those of previous rnd.

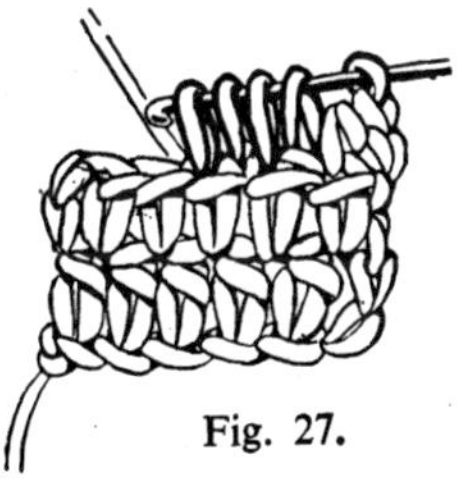

Fig. 27.

Fig. 29.

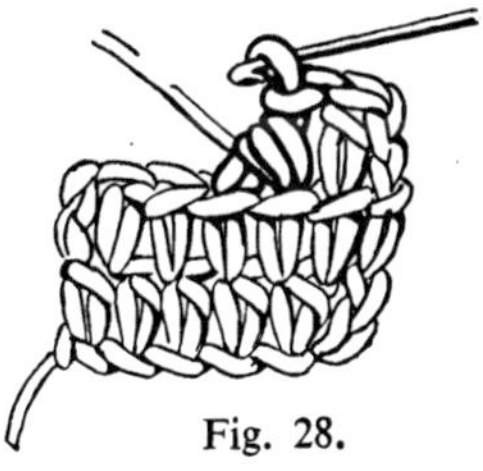

Fig. 28.

Fig. 30.

SOME PRETTY MATS

Materials. Mercer-Crochet No. 40 (20 gram). 2 balls selected colour. Milwards' Steel Crochet Hook No. 4.

MAT

Starting at centre, repeat Steps 1 to 9 of **rounds of half treble crochet** but do not break off at end of Step 9. Then repeat Step 10 until piece measures 17 in. in all. At end of last rnd, ss in next 2 sts.

EDGING

1st rnd. * 5 ch, dc in next hlf tr. Repeat from * all round, ending with 5 ch. **2nd rnd.** * Dc in next loop, 5 ch. Repeat from * all round, ending with 5 ch. Repeat the 2nd rnd 3 times more. Break off.

---

continued from next page

SECOND ROW (2nd row)

STEP 1. Thread over, insert the hook from the front under the 2 top loops of the 5th stitch from the hook (2nd stitch on previous row).

STEP 2. Repeat Steps 2 to 7 of First Row. Repeat the Second Row until you are familiar with this stitch. Break off.

Rows of Treble Crochet

(Abbreviation—tr)

Making a chain of 20 stitches for practice piece.

FIRST ROW (1st row)

STEP 1. Thread over, insert hook from the front under the 2 top threads of 4th ch from hook (Fig. 31).

STEP 2. Thread over and draw through stitch (st). There are now 3 loops on hook (Fig. 32).

STEP 3. Thread over (Fig. 32) and draw through 2 loops—2 loops remain on hook (Fig. 33).

STEP 4. Thread over again and draw through the 2 remaining loops —1 loop remains on hook. One treble chochet (tr) is now completed (Fig. 34).

STEP 5. For next treble crochet (tr), thread over, insert hook from the front under the 2 top loops of next stitch (st) and repeat Steps 2 to 5 until you have made a treble crochet (tr) in each chain.

STEP 6. At end of row, ch 3 (Fig. 35) and turn.

STEP 7. The turning 3 ch counts as the first treble crochet (tr) on next row. Therefore the first tr of each row is always missed.

When working a dbl tr—thread over twice.

When working a trip tr—thread over three times.

When working a quad tr—thread over four times.

When working a quint tr—thread over five times.

continued on previous page

Fig. 31.

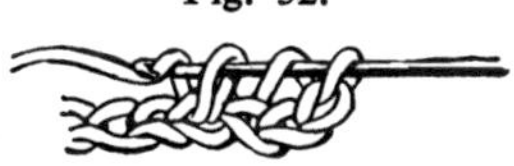
Fig. 32.

Fig. 33.

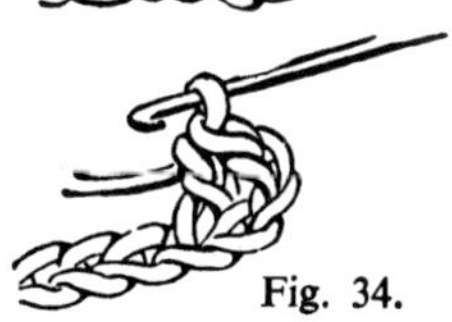
Fig. 34.

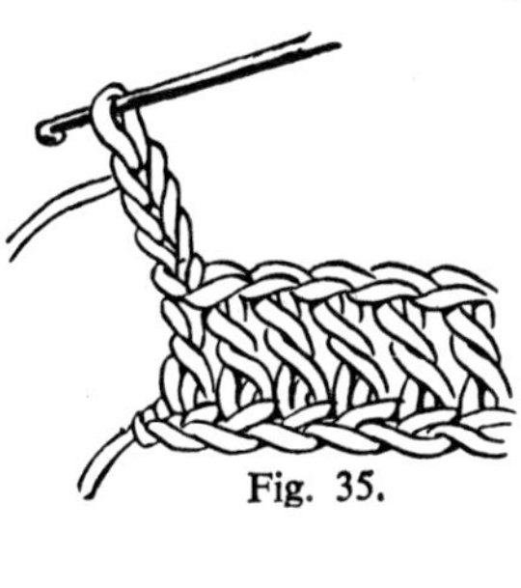
Fig. 35.

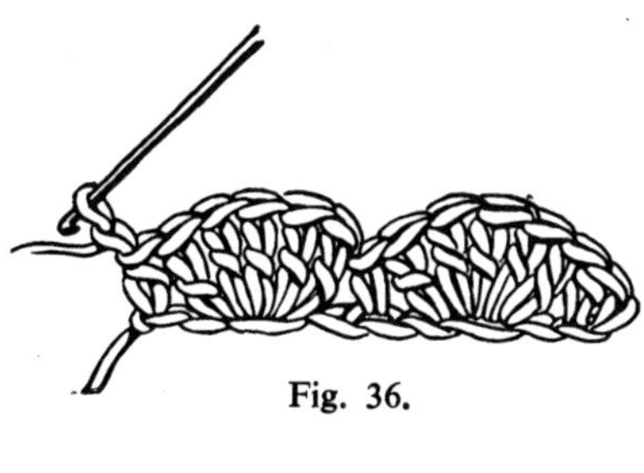
Fig. 36.

CROCHET * page 26

Shell Stitch Blouse

Photographs opposite.

Materials. Mercer-Crochet No. 40 (20 gram). 14 balls of selected colour. 2 Press Studs. 1 Milwards' Steel Crochet Hook No. 3. 1 Milwards' Steel Crochet Hook No. 4. Use double thread throughout.

Tension. 5 shells and 10 rows—2 in.

Measurements. Bust: 34 in. Width across back or front at underarm: 17 in. Length from shoulder to lower edge: 19½ in. Length of side seam: 10½ in.

BACK

Commence at lower edge using a No. 3 hook, make a ch 20 in. long (10 sts to 1 in.).

1st Row. 1 dc into 2nd ch from hook, * miss 2 ch, 5 tr into next ch (shell made), miss 2 ch, 1 dc into next ch (Fig. 36); repeat from * until there are 28 shells on row, ending with a dc. Cut off remaining ch, 3 ch, turn.

2nd Row. 2 tr into first dc (half shell), * 1 dc into centre tr of next shell, shell in next dc; repeat from * across, ending with 3 tr into last dc (half shell), 1 ch, turn.

3rd Row. 1 dc into first tr, * shell into next dc, 1 dc into centre tr of next shell; repeat from * across, ending with 1 dc into top of turning ch, 3 ch, turn.

Repeat 2nd and 3rd rows alternately until piece measures 5 in. Change to No. 4 hook and continue in pattern until piece measures 7 in. Change to No. 3 hook and continue in pattern until piece measures 10½ in. Place a marking thread at both ends of last row to indicate end of side seam. Continue in pattern until piece measures 19½ in. in all. Break off.

FRONT

Work exactly as for back until piece measures 18½ in. in all, ending with the 3rd row.

To Shape Neck

1st Row. Work in pattern until there are 9 shells completed, turn.

2nd Row. 1 ss into each of next 2 tr, 1 dc into centre tr of same shell, shell in next dc and complete row, 3 ch, turn.

3rd Row. Work half shell and 8 complete shells, turn.

4th Row. As 2nd row. Break off.

Miss 8 shells, attach thread in centre tr of next shell, 1 ch, 1 dc into same place as join and work across remainder of row to correspond with other side. Break off. Sew side seams to markings. Sew shoulder seams, leaving 2 in. free on left shoulder. Work dc along neck edge and shoulder opening. Sew on press studs. Work 3 rows of shells round armholes. Damp and press.

SHELL STITCH BLOUSE

LACE BLOUSE

Lace Blouse

Photograph opposite.

Materials. Mercer-Crochet No. 40 (20 gram). 7 balls selected colour. 16 buttons. Shoulder pads. Milwards' Steel Crochet Hook No. 4. (Slack workers could use a No. 4½ hook and tight workers a No. 3½.)

Tension. 5 blks=2 in.; 8 rows=1½ in.

Measurement. Bust—34 in.

Abbreviations. ch—chain; dc—double crochet; tr—treble; dbl tr—double treble; sp—space; blk—block.

BACK

Commence with 262 ch.

1st Row. 1 dc into 2nd ch from hook, 1 dc into each of the next 2 ch, * 3 ch, miss 3 ch, 1 dc into each of the next 3 ch; repeat from * to end of row (44 dc groups), 7 ch, turn.

2nd Row. * 3 dbl tr into next sp (blk made), 3 ch; repeat from * ending with 3 ch, 1 dbl tr into last dc (43 blks), 1 ch, turn.

3rd Row. * dc into next sp, 3 ch; repeat from * ending with 3 dc into last sp, 7 ch, turn.

Repeat 2nd and 3rd rows until piece measures 13 in., ending with a dbl tr row, 13 ch, turn.

Kimono Sleeves

1 dc into 2nd ch from hook, 1 dc into each of the next 2 ch, 3 ch, miss 3 ch, 1 dc into each of the next 3 ch, 3 ch, 3 dc into next sp and continue in pattern to end of row, 19 ch, turn.

Next Row. 1 dbl tr into 11th ch from hook, 1 dbl tr into each of the next 2 ch, 3 ch, miss 3 ch, 1 dbl tr into each of the next 3 ch, 3 ch, 3 dbl tr into next sp and continue in pattern to end of row (47 blks), 8 ch, turn.

To Shape Sleeves

1st Row. Work 3 dc in first sp, 3 ch and continue in pattern, ending with 3 dc in last sp, 6 ch, turn.

2nd Row. 1 dbl tr into 5th ch from hook, 1 dbl tr into next ch, 3 ch, 3 dbl tr in next sp and continue in pattern, ending with 3 dbl tr in turning 8 ch, 4 ch, turn.

3rd Row. 1 dc into 2nd ch from hook, 1 dc into each of the next 2 ch, 3 ch, 3 dc into next sp and continue in pattern to end of row, ending with 3 ch, 1 dc in top of turning ch, 7 ch, turn.

4th Row. 3 dbl tr into first sp, 3 ch and continue in pattern across, ending with 3 ch, 1 dbl tr into last dc (1 blk increased on each side), 1 ch, turn.

5th to 8th Row inclus. Work straight in pattern. Repeat these 8 rows 3 times more turning with 8 ch at end of each 8th row and omitting turning ch at end of last repeat. Work straight in pattern until piece measures 7 in., from start of sleeve, ending with a dc row and omitting turning ch (55 blks).

To Shape the Shoulders

1st Row. Ss across the first 3 sps, 7 ch, 3 dbl tr into next sp and continue in pattern across to last 3 sps, ending with 3 ch, miss next 2 dc, 1 dbl tr in next dc (3 blks decreased at each end), 1 ch, turn.

2nd Row. Work in pattern to end of row. Repeat the last 2 rows twice more.

LACE BLOUSE

(*continued*)

7th Row. Work same as first row of shoulder shaping, decreasing 4 blks at each end, 1 ch, turn.
8th Row. Work in pattern.
9th and 10th Rows. Repeat 7th and 8th rows.
11th Row. Work same as first row of shoulder, decreasing 4 blks at each end.
12th Row. Work in pattern. Fasten off.

Right Front

Commence with 136 ch. Work in pattern as for back having 23 dc groups on the first row and 22 dbl tr groups on the 2nd row, until piece measures 13 in., ending with a dbl tr row, 13 ch, turn.

Sleeve

Next Row. 1 dc into 2nd ch from hook, 1 dc into each of the next 2 ch, 3 ch, miss 3 ch, 1 dc into each of the next 3 ch, 3 ch, 3 dc into next sp and continue in pattern to end of row, 7 ch, turn.
Next Row. Work in pattern. There should now be 24 blks. Continue in pattern shaping sleeve edge same as on back until there are 28 blks. Work without increasing until piece measures 7 in., from start of sleeve, ending with a dc row.
To Shape Neck and Shoulders
1st Row. Decrease 3 blks at both ends of row.
2nd Row. Work in pattern.
3rd Row. Decrease 2 blks at neck edge and 3 blks at sleeve edge.
4th Row. Work in pattern.
5th Row. Decrease 1 blk at neck edge and 3 blks at sleeve edge.
6th Row. Work in pattern.
7th Row. Decrease 4 blks at sleeve edge.
8th Row. Work in pattern.
9th and 10th Rows. As 7th and 8th rows. Fasten off.

Left Front

Work same as Right Front up to sleeve, ending with a dc row, 19 ch, turn.
Next Row. 1 dbl tr into 11th ch from hook, 1 dbl tr into each of the next 2 ch, 3 ch, miss 3 ch, 1 dbl tr into each of the next 3 ch, 3 ch, 3 dbl tr into next sp and continue in pattern to end of row, 1 ch, turn.
Continue working to correspond with Right Front reversing all shapings.

Ruffle

Sew up shoulder seams. With right side of work facing, attach thread at lower right front edge.
1st Row. * 5 ch, 1 dc in next sp, 5 ch, 1 dc in same sp; repeat from * up right front edge, round neck and down left front edge, ending with 5 ch, 1 dc in corner at starting ch, 5 ch, turn.
2nd Row. 1 dc in next loop, * 5 ch, 1 dc in next loop; repeat from * all round, 5 ch, turn.
3rd Row. 1 dc in next loop, * 5 ch, 3 dbl tr in next loop, 5 ch, 1 dc in next loop; repeat from * all round, turn.
4th Row. * 5 ch, 1 dc into 3rd ch from hook (picot made), 2 ch, 1 dc into next loop; repeat from * all round. Fasten off. Sew up side seams. With right side facing, work 1 row of dc evenly along edge of sleeves. Pin out to measurements. Sew on buttons down front.

Sun Top

Materials. Mercer-Crochet No. 40 (20 gram). 10 balls selected colour. Milwards' Steel Crochet Hook No. 4. (Slack workers could use a No. $4\frac{1}{2}$ hook and tight workers a No. $3\frac{1}{2}$.)
Tension. 8 rows=1 in.
Measurement. Bust: 34 in.

Left Front
Commence with 266 ch.
1st Row. 1 dc into 2nd ch from hook, 1 dc into each of remaining ch, 6 ch, turn.
2nd Row. 1 tr into first dc, * miss 1 dc, 1 dc into next dc, miss 1 dc, 1 tr 3 ch 1 tr into next dc; repeat from * to end of row, 1 ch, turn.
3rd Row. I dc into first 3 ch sp, * 1 tr 3 ch 1 tr into next dc, 1 dc into next 3 ch sp; repeat from * ending with 1 tr 3 ch 1 tr into next dc, 1 dc into last sp, 6 ch, turn.
4th Row. 1 tr into first dc, * 1 dc into next 3 ch sp, 1 tr 3 ch 1 tr into next dc; repeat from * to end of row, 1 ch, turn. Repeat 3rd and 4th rows 19 times more.
43rd Row. As 3rd row.
44th Row. 1 tr into first dc, * 1 dc into next 3 ch sp, 1 tr 3 ch 1 tr into next dc; repeat from * ending with 1 dc into last 3 ch sp, 1 ch, turn.
45th Row. Ss to next 3 ch sp, 1 dc into sp, work in pattern to end of row. Repeat 44th and 45th rows 6 times more. Work in pattern for 6 more rows.
64th Row. 1 tr into first dc, * 1 dc into next 3 ch sp, 1 tr 3 ch 1 tr into next dc; repeat from * 8 times more, 1 dc into next 3 ch sp, 1 ch, turn.
65th Row. Ss to 3rd sp of 3 ch, 1 dc into sp, work in pattern to end of row, 6 ch, turn.
66th Row. 1 tr into first dc, * 1 dc into next 3 ch sp, 1 tr 3 ch 1 tr into next dc; repeat from * 3 times more, 1 dc into next 3 ch sp, 1 ch, turn.
67th Row. As 65th row.
68th Row. 1 tr into first dc, 1 dc into next 3 ch sp. Fasten off. Miss next 8 sps of 3 ch on 63rd row, join thread in next 3 ch sp and work 1 dc into this sp, work in pattern to end of row, 1 ch, turn.
Next Row. Work in pattern to last 3 ch sp, 1 ch, turn.
Next Row. Ss to next 3 ch sp, 1 dc into same sp, work in pattern to end of row, 1 ch, turn. Repeat last 2 rows 18 times more.
Next Row. Work in pattern to last 3 ch sp, 1 ch, turn.

SUN TOP

(*continued*)

Next Row. Ss to next 3 ch sp, 1 dc into same sp, work in pattern to 3rd last sp, 1 ch, turn. Repeat last 2 rows 4 times more.

Next Row. Ss to next 3 ch sp, 1 dc into same sp, 1 tr 3 ch 1 tr into next dc, 1 dc into next 3 ch sp. Fasten off. Work other front the same.

BACK

Commence with 207 ch.

1st Row. 1 dc into 2nd ch from hook, 1 dc into each ch, 6 ch, turn.

2nd Row. 1 tr into first dc, * miss 1 dc, 1 dc into next dc, miss 1 dc, 1 tr 3 ch 1 tr into next dc; repeat from * ending with miss 1 dc, 1 dc into next dc, 6 ch, turn.

3rd Row. 1 tr into first dc, * 1 dc into next sp, 1 tr 3 ch 1 tr into next dc; repeat from * ending with 1 dc into last sp, 2 ch, 1 tr into 3rd of turning ch, 1 ch, turn.

4th Row. 1 dc into 2 ch sp, work in pattern to end of row, 6 ch, turn.

5th Row. 1 tr into first dc, work in pattern to end of row, 5 ch, turn.

6th Row. 1 dc into first sp, work in pattern, ending with 1 dc into last sp, 2 ch, 1 tr into 3rd of turning ch, 1 ch, turn.

7th Row. 1 dc into 2 ch sp, work in pattern, ending with 1 dc into 3rd of turning ch, 6 ch, turn. Repeat last 3 rows 11 times more.

41st Row. As 5th row.

42nd Row. As 6th row.

43rd Row. Ss to 3rd sp of 3 ch, 1 dc into this sp, work in pattern to 3rd last sp of 3 ch, 1 dc into this sp, 1 ch, turn.

44th Row. Ss to first sp, 1 dc into this sp, work in pattern to last sp of 3 ch, 1 dc into this sp, 1 ch, turn. Repeat 44th row 5 times more, turning with 5 ch on last row.

50th Row. 1 dc into first 3 ch sp, work in pattern, ending with 1 dc into last 3 ch sp, 2 ch, 1 tr into last dc, 1 ch, turn.

51st Row. 1 dc into 2 ch sp, work in pattern, ending with 1 dc into 5 ch sp, 5 ch, turn. Repeat last 2 rows 27 times more, turning with 1 ch on last row.

Next Row. Ss to 3rd sp of 3 ch, 1 dc into this sp, work in pattern to 3rd last sp, 1 dc into this sp, 1 ch, turn.

Next Row. Ss to first sp, 1 dc into this sp, work in pattern to last sp, 1 dc into this sp, 1 ch, turn. Repeat last 2 rows 4 times more.

Next Row. As last row, omitting turning ch. Fasten off.

Sleeves

Commence with 186 ch.

1st Row. 1 dc into 2nd ch from hook, 1 dc into each ch, 6 ch, turn.

2nd Row. 1 tr into first dc, * miss 1 dc, 1 dc into next dc, miss 1 dc, 1 tr 3 ch 1 tr into next dc; repeat from * to end of row, 1 ch, turn.

3rd Row. 1 dc into 3 ch sp, * 1 tr 3 ch 1 tr into next dc, 1 dc into next 3 ch sp; repeat from * to end of row, 6 ch, turn.

SUN TOP
(continued)

4th Row. 1 tr into first dc, * 1 dc into next 3 ch sp, 1 tr 3 ch 1 tr into next dc; repeat from * to end of row, 1 ch, turn.
Repeat 3rd and 4th rows 10 times more, then 3rd row once more, turning with 1 ch.

26th Row. Ss to 3rd sp of 3 ch, 1 dc into this sp, work in pattern to 3rd last sp, 1 dc into this sp, 1 ch, turn.

27th Row. Ss to first sp of 3 ch, 1 dc into sp, work in pattern to last 3 ch sp, 1 dc into this sp, 1 ch, turn. Repeat 27th row 8 times more, turning with 6 ch on last row.

36th Row. 1 tr into first dc, work in pattern, ending with 1 tr 3 ch 1 tr into last dc, 1 ch, turn.

37th Row. As 3rd row, turning with 1 ch.

38th Row. As 27th row, turning with 6 ch.
Repeat last 3 rows 6 times more, turning with 1 ch on last row. Repeat 27th row 19 times more, omitting turning ch on last row. Fasten off.

CUFF
Join thread in first of foundation ch.

1st Row. 6 ch, 1 tr into same place as join, * miss next ch, 1 dc into next ch, miss next ch, 1 tr 3 ch 1 tr into next ch; repeat from * to end of row, 1 ch, turn.

2nd Row. 1 dc into first 3 ch sp, work in pattern to end of row, 1 ch, turn.

3rd Row. Ss to first 3 ch sp, 1 dc into sp, work in pattern to last 3 ch sp, 1 dc into last sp, 1 ch, turn. Repeat 3rd row 9 times more, omitting turning ch on last row. Fasten off.
Join thread in same place as join of cuff and work a row of dc all round edge of cuff. Fasten off.
Work another sleeve the same.

COLLAR
Commence with 370 ch.

1st Row. 1 dc into 2nd ch from hook, 1 dc into each ch, 6 ch, turn.

2nd Row. As 2nd row of sleeve.

3rd Row. As 3rd row of sleeve, turning with 1 ch.

4th Row. Ss to 2nd sp of 3 ch, 1 dc into this sp, work in pattern to 2nd last sp, 1 dc into this sp, 1 ch, turn.
Repeat 4th row 9 times more.
Fasten off. Join thread in first of foundation ch and work a row of dc round the outer edge.

To Make-Up
Sew up side and shoulder seams, sew up sleeve seams and insert into armhole. Sew on collar.
Damp and press, folding collar and cuffs to right side.

Now we are introducing you to pattern in this

Bag and Bandeau Set

Materials. Mercer-Crochet No. 40 (20 gram). 9 balls selected colour. Piece of lining to match crochet cotton. Piece of canvas. 2 rings. 2 press studs. One piece of elastic. Milwards' Steel Crochet Hook No. $2\frac{1}{2}$. Use 3 threads throughout.

Tension. 11 rows=1 in. approximately.

Measurement of Bag. $10\frac{1}{2}$ in. $\times$ $12\frac{1}{2}$ in.

BAG

Commence with 161 ch.

1st Row. 1 dc into 2nd ch from hook 1 dc into each of remaining ch (160 dc), 1 ch, turn.

2nd Row. 1 dc into each dc, 1 ch, turn.

Repeat 2nd row 20 times more, turning with 4 ch on last row.

23rd Row. 3 tr into first dc leaving the last loop of each on hook, thread over and pull through all loops on hook (a cluster made), * miss 2 dc, 1 dc into next dc, 4 ch, 1 cluster into same place as last dc; repeat from * ending with miss 2 dc, 1 dc into next dc, 4 ch, turn.

24th Row. 1 dc into sp of 4 ch of last cluster, * 4 ch, 1 cluster into same place as last dc, 1 dc into sp of 4 ch of next cluster; repeat from * to end of row, 4 ch, turn.

25th Row. As 24th row, turning with 1 ch.

26th Row. 1 dc into first dc, 3 dc into each 4 ch sp, 1 ch, turn.
Repeat 2nd row 58 times more, turning with 4 ch on last row.
Repeat 23rd to 26th row once more.
Repeat 2nd row 21 times more. Do not turn at end of last row but work along row-ends as follows: 1 dc into each row-end. Fasten off. Join thread at opposite end and work 1 dc into each row-end. Fasten off.

FLAP

Commence with 105 ch.

1st Row. 1 cluster into 5th ch from hook, * miss 4 ch, 1 dc into next ch, 4 ch, 1 cluster into same place as last dc; repeat from * ending with miss 4 ch, 1 dc into next ch, 4 ch, turn.

2nd and 3rd Rows. As 24th row of bag turning with 4 ch on last row.

4th Row. 1 dc into sp of 4 ch, turn, 5 dc over last 4 ch, 1 dc into dc of row-end, 3 dc over turning ch of next row-end, 5 dc over next 4 ch, * 1 dc into same place as cluster, 3 dc over next 4 ch; repeat from * 17 times more, 1 dc into same place as next cluster, 5 dc over next 4 ch, 1 dc into same place as next cluster, 3 dc over next 4 ch, 1 dc into dc of row-end, 5 dc over next 4 ch, 4 dc over each of next 19 loops of 4 ch.

5th Row. 1 dc into each dc working 3 dc into 3rd of each 5 dc at corners.

6th Row. 1 dc into each dc working 3 dc into 2nd of each 3 dc at corners.
Repeat 6th row 3 times more, ending with 1 ss into first dc. Fasten off.

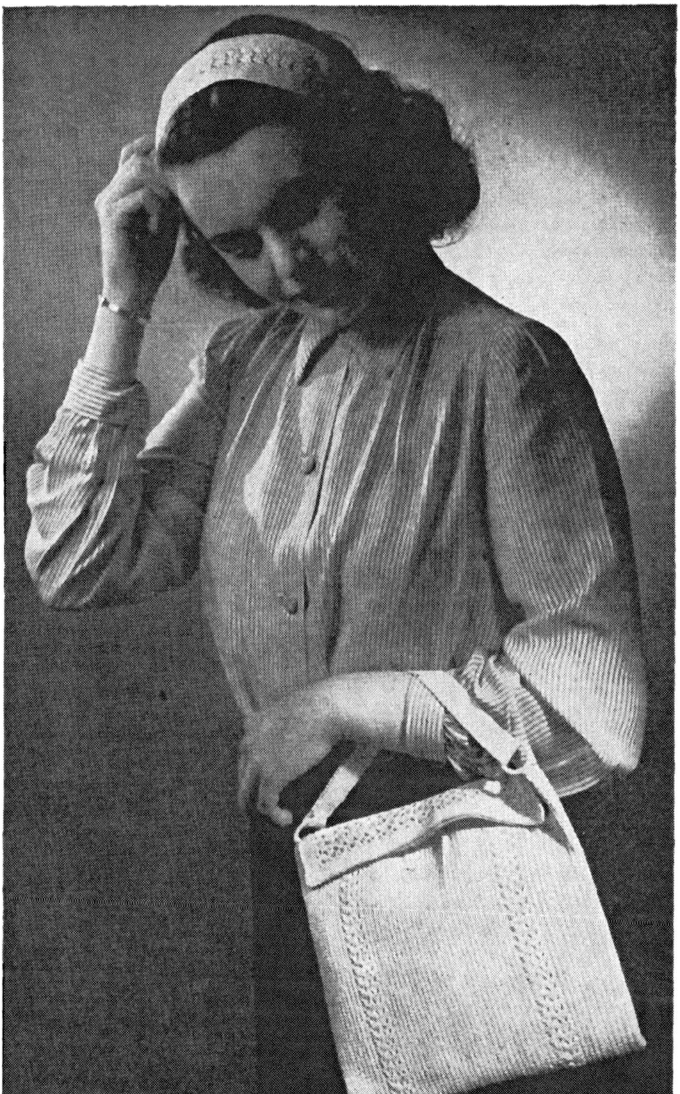

BAG AND BANDEAU SET

BAG AND BANDEAU SET
(continued)

HANDLE
Make a chain 12½ in. long.

1st Row. 1 dc into 2nd ch from hook, 1 dc into each ch, 3 dc into last ch, 1 dc into other half of each foundation ch, 2 dc into same place as first dc.

2nd Row. I dc into each dc working 3 dc into centre dc at each point. Repeat 2nd row twice more, ending with 1 ss into first dc. Fasten off. Work a row of dc over each of the two rings.

To Make-Up
Insert canvas between lining then slip stitch to wrong side of bag. Fold bag and over-cast edges together. Line flap in same manner and sew to back of bag. Sew one ring at each end of top of bag. Line handle and sew an end over each ring. Sew on press studs.

BANDEAU
Work same as flap for first 3 rows, omitting turning ch on last row.

4th Row. 4 dc into same place as last dc, * 3 dc over next 4 ch, 1 dc into same place as cluster; repeat from * 19 times more, 5 dc over next 4 ch, 4 dc over each of next 20 loops of 4 ch.

5th Row. 1 dc into each dc working 5 dc into centre dc at each point. Repeat 5th row 6 times more, ending with 1 ss into first dc. Fasten off. Sew elastic to Bandeau.

Starting to Show Off! How to do Irish Crochet.

Irish Crochet Tablecloth

Photographs opposite.

Materials. Mercer-Crochet No. 40 (20 gram). 72 balls of selected colour. Milwards' Steel Crochet Hook No. 4.

Size of Motif. 4 in. square and 5½ in. diagonally.

Measurement. 72 × 110 in. (approx.).

First Motif. Commence with 8 ch, join with ss to form a ring.

1st Row. 1 ch, 18 dc into ring, 1 ss into first dc.

2nd Row. 1 ch, 1 dc into same place as ss, * 5 ch, miss 2 dc, 1 dc into next dc; repeat from * all round, join with ss into first dc. (6 loops.)

3rd Row. 1 ss into first loop, into each loop work 1 dc 1 hlf tr 5 tr 1 hlf tr and 1 dc (6 petals).

4th Row. * 7 ch, insert hook into next loop (from back of work), pass hook across front of dc and insert in following loop (from front of work), thread over and draw loop through, thread over and draw through both loops on hook; repeat from * all round (6 loops).

Feeling ambitious? How about trying your hand at this beautiful tablecloth? It's one of the loveliest you'll ever see . . . something you'll cherish for ever.

IRISH CROCHET TABLECLOTH

(*continued*)

5th Row. 1 ss into first loop, into each loop work 1 dc 1 hlf tr 1 tr 7 dbl tr 1 tr 1 hlf tr and 1 dc.

6th Row. 1 ss into each of first 4 sts of next petal, 1 ch, 1 dc into same place as last ss, * 5 ch, 1 dc into 4th ch from hook (picot made), 2 ch, picot, 1 ch, miss 5 dbl tr, 1 dc into next dbl tr, 1 ch, picot, 2 ch, picot, 1 ch, 1 dc into first dbl tr of next petal; repeat from * all round (12 loops).

7th Row. Ss to centre of next loop (between picots), 4 ch, 1 dbl tr into same place as last ss, 1 ch, picot, 2 ch, picot, 1 ch, then, holding back on hook the last loop of each dbl tr, make 2 dbl tr in same place where last dbl tr was made, thread over and draw through all loops on hook (2 dbl tr cluster made), * 1 ch, picot, 2 ch, picot, 1 ch, 1 dc between picots of next loop, 9 ch, 1 dc between picots of next loop, 1 ch, picot, 2 ch, picot, 1 ch, miss picot of next loop and the following ch, work a 2 dbl tr cluster in next ch, 1 ch, picot, 2 ch, picot, 1 ch, 2 dbl tr cluster in same place as last cluster; repeat from * all round, join to top of first dbl tr.

8th Row. Ss to centre of next loop, 4 ch, 1 dbl tr into same place as last ss, 1 ch, picot, 2 ch, picot, 1 ch, 2 dbl tr cluster into same place as last dbl tr, * 1 ch, picot, 2 ch, picot, 1 ch, 1 dc into next loop, 3 ch, into 9 ch loop work (a 3 dbl tr cluster, picot) 3 times and a 3 dbl tr cluster, 3 ch, 1 dc into next loop, 1 ch, picot, 2 ch, picot, 1 ch, miss the picot of next loop and the following ch, make a 2 dbl tr cluster in next ch, 1 ch, picot, 2 ch, picot, 1 ch, 2 dbl tr cluster into same place as last cluster; repeat from * all round, join.

9th Row. Ss to centre of next loop, 5 ch, picot, 1 ch, 1 dbl tr into same loop, 1 ch, picot, 1 ch, 1 dbl tr into same loop, * 1 ch, picot, 1 ch, 1 dbl tr between picots of next loop, 1 ch, picot, 1 ch, 1 dbl tr into next 3 ch sp, 1 ch, picot, 1 ch, miss next cluster, 1 tr into top of each of next 2 clusters, 1 ch, picot, 1 ch, miss next cluster, 1 dbl tr into next 3 ch sp, 1 ch, picot, 1 ch, 1 dbl tr between picots of next loop, 1 ch, picot, 1 ch, into next loop (between picots) make 5 dbl tr with 1 ch picot and 1 ch between each dbl tr; repeat from * all round, join with ss to 4th of 5 ch.

10th Row. 17 ch, 1 dbl tr into same place as ss, * (1 ch, picot, 1 ch, 1 dbl tr into next dbl tr) 4 times, 1 ch, picot, 1 ch, miss 1 tr, 1 dbl tr into next tr, (1 ch, picot, 1 ch, 1 dbl tr into next dbl tr) 4 times, 1 ch, picot, 1 ch, into next dbl tr work 1 dbl tr 13 ch and 1 dbl tr; repeat from * all round, join and break off.

Second Motif

Work as for first motif until 9th row is completed.

10th Row. 10 ch (to count as dbl tr and 6 ch), 1 ss into centre ch of corner loop on first motif, 6 ch, 1 dbl tr into same place as ss on second motif, (3 ch, 1 ss into corresponding picot on first motif, 2 ch, 1 dc into

IRISH CROCHET TABLECLOTH
(continued)

2nd ch of last 3 ch, thus joining picots, 1 ch, 1 dbl tr into next dbl tr on second motif) 4 times, 3 ch, 1 ss into next picot on first motif, 2 ch, 1 dc into 2nd ch of last 3 ch, 1 ch, miss 1 tr, 1 dbl tr into next tr on second motif, (3 ch, 1 ss into next picot on first motif, 2 ch, 1 dc into 2nd ch of last 3 ch, 1 ch, 1 dbl tr into next dbl tr on second motif) 5 times, 6 ch, 1 ss into centre ch of corner loop on first motif, 6 ch, 1 dbl tr in same place as last dbl tr on second motif. Complete as for first motif (no more joinings). Break off. Make 488 motifs, joining adjacent sides as second motif was joined to first (where 4 corners meet, join 3rd and 4th corners to joining of previous 2 corners).

Join motifs in the following order:

1st Row. 1 motif. **2nd Row.** 3 motifs. (1 motif extending on each side of previous row.)

3rd Row. 5 motifs. **4th Row.** 7 motifs.
Continue thus, having 2 more motifs on each row until there are 25 motifs on row. Make 7 more rows of 25 motifs each, having 1 motif extend beyond left edge and having 1 motif less on right side. Now make 2 motifs less on each row (1 motif less on each side until last row has 1 motif).

Round Luncheon Set

Photograph on page 41.

Materials. Mercer-Crochet No. 40 (20 gram). 3 balls selected colour. Milwards' Steel Crochet Hook No. 4. Commence with 12 ch, join with ss to form a ring.

1st Row. 3 ch, 23 tr into ring, join with ss to 3rd of 3 ch.

2nd Row. 9 ch, * miss 1 tr, 1 dbl tr into next tr, 5 ch; repeat from * ending with 1 ss into 4th of 9 ch.

3rd Row. Into each 5 ch loop work 1 dc 1 hlf tr 3 tr 1 hlf tr and 1 dc, 1 ss into first dc.

4th Row. Ss to centre tr of group, 1 dc into centre tr, * 9 ch, drop loop from hook, insert hook in 5th ch and draw dropped loop through, 3 ch, 7 tr into loop just made, 3 ch, 1 ss into base of 5 ch loop, 4 ch, 1 dc into centre tr of next loop; repeat from * omitting 1 dc at end of last repeat, 1 ss into first dc. Break off.

5th Row. Attach thread to centre tr on any ring, * 11 ch, 1 dc into centre tr of next ring; repeat from * ending with 11 ch, 1 ss into same place as ss. **6th Row.** 3 ch, * 1 tr into each of next 5 ch, 3 tr into centre ch, 1 tr into each of next 5 ch, 1 tr into next dc; repeat from * join with ss into 3rd of 3 ch. **7th Row.** 1 ss into each of next 6 tr, 3 ch, 1 tr into each of next 2 tr, * 11 ch, 1 tr into each tr of next 3 tr group; repeat from * ending with 11 ch, 1 ss into 3rd of 3 ch. **8th Row.** 3 ch, 1 tr into same place as ss, * 1 tr into next tr, 2 tr into next tr, 7 ch, 1 dc into next loop, 7 ch, 2 tr into next tr; repeat from * ending with 7 ch, 1 ss into 3rd of 3 ch. **9th Row.** 3 ch, * 1 tr into each of next 4 tr, (5 ch, 1 dc into next loop) twice, 5 ch, 1 tr into next tr; repeat from * omitting 1 tr at end of last repeat, 1 ss into 3rd of 3 ch. **10th Row.** 3 ch, 1 tr into each of next 4 tr, * 9 ch, 1 dc into centre loop, 9 ch, 1 tr into each of next 5 tr; repeat from * omitting 5 tr at end of last repeat, 1 ss into 3rd of 3 ch. **11th Row.** 3 ch, 1 tr into each of next 4 tr, * 5 ch, 1 dc into next loop, 9 ch, 1 dc into next loop, 5 ch, 1 tr into each of next 5 tr; repeat from * omitting 5 tr at end of last repeat, 1 ss into 3rd of 3 ch.

12th Row. 3 ch, 1 tr into each of next 4 tr, * 7 ch, 1 dc into centre loop, 7 ch, 1 tr into each of next 5 tr; repeat from * omitting 5 tr at end of last repeat, 1 ss into 3rd of 3 ch. **13th Row.** 3 ch, 1 tr into each of next 4 tr, * 5 ch, 1 dc into next loop, 9 ch, 1 dc into next loop, 5 ch, 1 tr into each of next 5 tr; repeat from * omitting 5 tr at end of last repeat, 1 ss into 3rd of 3 ch.

14th Row. 3 ch, 1 tr into each of next 4 tr, * 8 ch, 1 dc into centre loop, 8 ch, 1 tr into each of next 5 tr; repeat from * omitting 5 tr at end of last repeat, 1 ss into 3rd of 3 ch.

15th Row. 3 ch, 1 tr into each of next 4 tr, * 7 ch, 5 dbl tr into next dc, 7 ch, 1 tr into each of next 5 tr; repeat from * omitting 5 tr at end of last repeat, 1 ss into 3rd of 3 ch.

16th Row. 3 ch, 1 tr into each of next 4 tr, * 2 ch, 1 tr into next sp, 9 ch, 1 dbl tr into each of next 5 dbl tr leaving the last loop of each on hook, thread over and draw through all loops on hook (a cluster made), 9 ch, 1 tr into next sp, 2 ch, 1 tr into each of next 5 tr; repeat from * omitting 5 tr at end of last repeat, 1 ss into 3rd of 3 ch.

17th Row. 3 ch, 1 tr into each of next 4 tr, * 2 ch, 1 tr into next tr, 2 ch, 1 tr into next loop, 3 ch, 1 tr into same loop, 3 ch, into next loop work 1 tr 3 ch and 1 tr, 2 ch, 1 tr into next tr, 2 ch, 1 tr into each of next 5 tr; repeat from * omitting 5 tr at end of last repeat, 1 ss into 3rd of 3 ch.

18th Row. 3 ch, 1 tr into next tr, * into next tr work 1 tr 2 ch and 1 tr, 1 tr into each of next 2 tr, 1 ch, 1 tr into next tr, 2 ch, 1 tr into next tr, (3 ch, 1 tr into next tr) 3 times, 2 ch, 1 tr into next tr, 1 ch, 1 tr into each of next 2 tr; repeat from * omitting 2 tr at end of last repeat, 1 ss into 3rd of 3 ch.

19th Row. 4 ch, 1 dbl tr into each of next 2 tr, * 2 ch, 1 dbl tr into sp, 2 ch, 1 dbl tr into each of next 3 tr, 3 ch, miss 1 tr, 1 dbl tr into next tr, 3 ch, 1 dbl tr into next tr, 3 dbl tr into next sp, 1 dbl tr into next tr, 3 ch, 1 dbl tr into next tr, 3 ch, miss 1 tr, 1 dbl tr into each of next 3 tr; repeat from * omitting 3 dbl tr at end of last repeat, 1 ss into 4th of 4 ch.

20th Row. 4 ch, 1 dbl tr into each of next 2 dbl tr, * (3 ch, 1 dbl tr into next sp) twice, 3 ch, 1 dbl tr into each of next 3 dbl tr, 1 ch, 1 tr into next dbl tr, 5 ch, 1 dc into centre dbl tr of next dbl tr group, 5 ch, 1 dc into next dbl tr, 1 ch, 1 dbl tr into each of next 3 dbl tr; repeat from * omitting 3 dbl tr at end of last repeat, 1 ss into 4th of 4 ch.

21st Row. 4 ch, 1 dbl tr into each of next 2 dbl tr, * (5 ch, 1 dbl tr into next sp) 3 times, 3 ch, 1 dbl tr into each of next 3 dbl tr, 3 ch, miss 1 sp, 1 dc into next loop, 7 ch, 1 dc into next loop, 3 ch, 1 dbl tr into each of next 3 dbl tr; repeat from * omitting 3 dbl tr at end of last repeat, 1 ss into 4th of 4 ch.

22nd Row. 3 ch, 1 tr into each of next 2 dbl tr, * 6 tr into each of next 4 loops, 1 tr into each of next 3 dbl tr, 5 ch, 1 dc into centre loop, 5 ch, 1 tr into each of next 3 dbl tr; repeat from * omitting 3 tr at end of last repeat, 1 ss into 3rd of 3 ch.

23rd Row. 5 ch, 2 trip tr into same place as last ss leaving the last loop of each on hook, thread over and draw through all loops on hook (a cluster made), * (5 ch, miss 2 tr, 3 trip tr cluster into next tr) 9 times, 5 ch, miss 1 tr, 1 cluster into last tr, 1 cluster into first tr of next tr group; repeat from * omitting 1 cluster at end of last repeat, 1 ss into top of first cluster.

24th Row. Ss to centre of next 5 ch, * 6 ch, 1 ss into 3rd ch from hook (picot made), 3 ch, 1 dc into next loop; repeat from * all round, join and break off.

Glass Jackets and Mats

Materials. Mercer-Crochet No. 40 (20 gram). 2 balls selected colour. 2 balls contrasting colour. Milwards' Steel Crochet Hook No. 2½. (Slack workers could use a No. 3 hook and tight workers a No. 2.)

The above quantity is sufficient for 3 glass jackets and 3 mats.

Abbreviations. ch—chain; ss—slip stitch; dc—double crochet—tr—treble; sp—space.

Use double thread throughout.

GLASS JACKET BOTTOM

With selected colour, commence with 4 ch.

1st Row. 11 tr into 4th ch from hook, 1 ss into top of starting ch.

2nd Row. 3 ch, 1 tr into same place as ss, 2 tr into each tr, 1 ss into 3rd of 3 ch.

3rd Row. 3 ch, * 2 tr into next tr, 1 tr into next tr; repeat from * ending with 2 tr into last tr, 1 ss into 3rd of 3 ch.

4th Row. 3 ch, 1 tr into each tr increasing 12 times evenly all round (to increase, work 2 tr into 1 tr), 1 ss into 3rd of 3 ch. Repeat 4th row until piece measures same as bottom of glass.

SIDE

1st Row. Drop selected colour, attach contrasting colour, 1 ch, 1 dc into back loop of each tr, 1 ss into first dc.

2nd Row. Drop contrasting colour, pick up selected colour, 1 ch, 1 dc into each dc, 1 ss into first dc.

3rd Row. 1 ch, 1 dc into each dc, 1 ss into first dc.

4th Row. Drop selected colour, pick up contrasting colour, 1 ch, 1 dc into same place as ss, * 1 dc into next dc on previous contrasting colour row 3 rows below (a long dc made), miss 1 dc on 3rd row, 1 dc into next dc on 3rd row, miss 1 dc of previous contrasting colour; repeat from * ending with 1 ss into first dc. Repeat 2nd, 3rd and 4th rows until side measures $2\frac{1}{4}$ in., ending with 4th row. Fasten off.

Attach contrasting colour to a free loop on last row of bottom and work 1 dc into each tr, having wrong side of dc facing bottom, 1 ss into first dc. Fasten off.

MATS

Bottom. With selected colour, commence with 4 ch.

1st Row. 11 tr into the 4th ch from hook, 1 ss into top of starting ch.

2nd Row. Drop selected colour, attach contrasting colour, 1 ch, 1 dc into same place as ss, * 2 dc into next tr, 1 dc into next tr; repeat from * ending with 2 dc into next tr, 1 ss into first dc.

3rd Row. Drop contrasting colour, pick up selected colour, 3 ch, 1 tr into each dc increasing 12 times in row (to increase work 2 tr into same place), 1 ss into 3rd of 3 ch.

4th Row. Drop selected colour, pick up contrasting colour, 1 ch, 1 dc into each tr increasing 6 times in row, 1 ss into first dc.

Repeat 3rd and 4th rows alternately until piece measures about $\frac{1}{4}$ in. larger than bottom of glass, ending with the 3rd row.

Edging

1st Row. Drop selected colour, pick up contrasting colour, work 1 dc into back loop of each tr increasing 8 times in row, 1 ss into first dc.

2nd Row. Drop contrasting colour, pick up selected colour, 1 dc into same place as ss, * 5 ch, 3 tr into same place as last dc, miss 3 dc, 1 dc into next dc; repeat from * omitting 1 dc at end of last repeat, 1 ss into first dc. Fasten off selected colour.

3rd Row. Pick up contrasting colour, * 5 dc into 5 ch loop, 1 dc into each tr; repeat from * ending with 1 ss into first dc. Fasten off.

Attach contrasting colour to other half of loop of last row of bottom and work edging same as previous edging omitting increases on first row. Fasten off.

CROCHET * page 44

Tray Cover

(See top photograph opposite)

Materials. Mercer-Crochet No. 40 (20 gram). 4 balls selected colour. Milwards' Steel Crochet Hook No. 4.

Size of Motif. $1\frac{1}{4}$ in. square.

Measurement. $12\frac{1}{2} \times 18\frac{1}{2}$ in.

First Motif

Commence at centre with 12 ch, join with ss to form a ring.

1st Row. 1 ch, into ring work 24 dc, 1 ss into first dc.

2nd Row. 4 ch, 2 dbl tr into same place as ss leaving the last loop of each on hook, thread over and draw through all loops on hook (cluster made), * 5 ch, miss 1 dc, 3 dbl tr into next dc leaving the last loop of each on hook, thread over and draw through all loops on hook (another cluster); repeat from * ending with 5 ch, 1 ss into top of first cluster.

3rd Row. 1 ss into each of next 2 ch, 1 dc into same loop, * 5 ch, into next loop work 1 cluster 7 ch and 1 cluster, (5 ch, 1 dc into next loop) twice; repeat from * omitting 1 dc at end of last repeat, 1 ss into first dc. Break off.

Second Motif

Work first 2 rows as for first motif.

3rd Row. 1 ss into each of next 2 ch, 1 dc into loop, 5 ch, 1 cluster into next loop, 3 ch, 1 dc into corresponding loop on first motif, 3 ch, 1 cluster into same loop as last cluster on second motif, 2 ch, 1 dc into corresponding loop on first motif, 2 ch, 1 dc into next loop on second motif and complete as for first motif, joining next 3 loops to corresponding loops of first motif as before.

Make 9 rows of 14 motifs, joining them as second motif was joined to first motif (where 4 corners meet, join 3rd and 4th corners to joining of previous 2 corners).

EDGING

1st Row. Attach thread to free corner loop, 4 ch and complete a cluster in same loop, 5 ch, 1 cluster into same loop, * 5 ch, 1 dc into next loop, 5 ch, into next loop work 1 cluster 5 ch 1 cluster, 5 ch, 1 dc into next loop, 5 ch, into joining of motifs work 1 cluster 5 ch and 1 cluster; repeat from * making 1 cluster 5 ch and 1 cluster into each corner loop, ending with 5 ch, 1 ss into top of first cluster.

2nd Row. 1 ss into corner loop, 4 ch and complete cluster, (5 ch, 1 cluster into same place) twice, * 5 ch, 1 dc into next loop, 2 ch, 1 dc into next loop, 5 ch, into next loop work 1 cluster 5 ch and 1 cluster; repeat from * making (1 cluster, 5 ch) twice and 1 cluster into each corner loop. Join and break off.

TRAY COVER

EDGINGS (*see next page*)

4 3 2 1

Edgings

See photograph on previous page.

Materials. Mercer-Crochet No. 60 (20 gram). 1 ball selected colour. Milwards' Steel Crochet Hook No. 5.

No. 1

1st Row. Commence with 10 ch, 1 tr into 6th ch from hook, 1 ch, miss 1 ch, 1 tr into next ch, 1 ch, miss 1 ch, into last ch work 1 tr 1 ch and 1 tr, 4 ch, turn.

2nd Row. Miss first tr, (1 tr into next tr, 1 ch) twice, 1 tr into next tr, 5 tr into last sp, 5 ch, turn.

3rd Row. 1 tr into first tr, (1 ch, miss 1 tr, 1 tr into next tr) twice, 1 ch, 1 tr into next sp, 4 ch, turn. Repeat 2nd and 3rd rows for length required.

No. 2

Make a chain slightly longer than length required.

1st Row. 1 dc into 2nd ch from hook, * 5 ch, 1 dc into each of next 5 ch; repeat from * until row is length required, ending with 5 ch, 1 dc into next ch (be sure to have an odd number of loops). Cut off remaining ch, turn.

2nd Row. 1 ss into next dc, 1 ss into loop, 4 ch, 2 dbl tr into same loop leaving the last loop of each on hook, thread over and pull through all loops on hook (a cluster made), 8 ch, 3 dbl tr into same loop leaving the last loop of each on hook, thread over and pull through all loops on hook (a 3 dbl tr cluster), * 3 ch, 1 dc into next loop, 3 ch, into next loop work a 3 dbl tr cluster 8 ch and a 3 dbl tr cluster; repeat from * across, 1 ch, turn.

3rd Row. * Into next 8 ch loop work (2 dc, 3 ch) 4 times and 2 dc, 2 dc into each of next 2 sps; repeat from * across. Fasten off.

No. 3

Commence with 11 ch.

1st Row. 3 dbl tr into 11th ch from hook leaving the last loop of each on hook, thread over and pull through all loops on hook (a cluster made), 5 ch, turn.

2nd Row. 1 tr into top of cluster, 10 ch, turn.

3rd Row. Make a 3 dbl tr cluster into top of last tr, 5 ch, turn. Repeat 2nd and 3rd rows for length required, ending with a 3 dbl tr cluster, 5 ch and work along one long edge as follows: * into next 5 ch loop work a 3 dbl tr cluster 5 ch and a 3 dbl tr cluster; repeat from * across, 5 ch, 1 ss in base of first cluster made. Now work along opposite edge as follows: * into next 10 ch loop work (3 dc, 3 ch) 3 times and 3 dc, 1 dc between loops; repeat from last * across. Fasten off.

No. 4

Make a chain slightly longer than length required.

1st Row. 1 tr into 6th ch from hook, * 1 ch, miss 1 ch, 1 tr into next ch; repeat from * until row is length required. Cut off remaining ch, 3 ch, turn.

2nd Row. * 1 tr into next 1 ch sp, 1 tr into next tr; repeat from * ending with 1 tr into last sp, 1 tr into top of turning ch, 4 ch, turn.

3rd Row. Miss first 2 tr, 1 tr into next tr, * 1 ch, miss 1 tr, 1 tr into next tr; repeat from * ending with 1 ch, miss 1 tr, 1 tr into top of turning ch 1 ch, turn.

4th Row. Into each sp across work 1 dc 5 ch 1 dc. Fasten off.

☆ TATTING ☆
OR *Frivolité*

FRIVOLITÉ is the charming name that the French give to the needlework we know as 'tatting'—and a very much more appropriate word it is! The art of tatting seems to have originated on the Continent, where an early form of it was very popular in the elegant, second half of the eighteenth century and, when it crossed the Channel, prim English ladies possibly considered that the adoption of the Continental title might provoke unseemly misunderstanding. Certainly 'Miss Emma is at her frivolity' would have sounded an altogether indecorous statement to an early Victorian mamma—and so tatting it became; but tatting is hardly descriptive of the exquisite, frothy result a good needlewoman produces with the little instrument called a tatting shuttle.

It was the Victorians, about a hundred years ago, who first revived the art and considerably improved the process of working. After the first world war, however, all things Victorian, good, bad or indifferent were lumped together and classed as 'stuffy.' As a result many fine needlework arts were forgotten, until a few years ago women began to rediscover what might be called the more feminine handicrafts. So it was, that about the time when the so-called 'new look' began to turn the fashion world upside down, tatting, one of the most enchanting of such handicrafts, was revived and began to enjoy a new lease of life. It was smart Frenchwomen who first saw the many exciting possibilities of tatting for present-day use, but they were speedily followed by the fashionable in England and America, and this fascinating form of needlework has become, for the third time in a hundred and fifty years, a modish pastime, and it looks likely to be an enduring vogue—as it deserves to be. It is a simple enough process and, with practice, proficiency comes quite soon even to the not so neat fingered: considering the elaborate effect obtained this is decidedly gratifying. In the following pages, full and clear instructions are given on tatting, followed by a number of examples and attractive tatted designs adapted to a variety of different purposes.

How to Tat

THREADS

Use Mercer-Crochet in No. 20, 40, 60 or 70. All the articles illustrated in this book can be worked in any of these four sizes.*

* *When instructions are given for fine work in No. 60 and No. 70, practically the identical results will be achieved with either number.*

SHUTTLES

Shuttles are made in various materials, such as Bone, Tortoise Shell and Steel. Choose one that is not more than 2½ in. long if possible; longer ones are more clumsy and make the work slower to do.

WIND THE SHUTTLE

Wind thread round the bobbin in centre of shuttle. If there is a hole in centre of bobbin, insert thread through the hole and tie a knot. Do not wind thread beyond the edge of the shuttle.

Hold the Shuttle in the Right Hand

STEP 1. Hold shuttle in right hand. Unwind shuttle so that the shuttle thread is about 15 in. long (Fig. 37).

STEP 2. Hold shuttle so that a pointed end is facing the left hand and the thread coming from the back of the bobbin (Fig. 37).

STEP 3. Grasp flat side between thumb and forefinger in a horizontal position, holding the other three fingers on a level with the forefinger (Fig. 37).

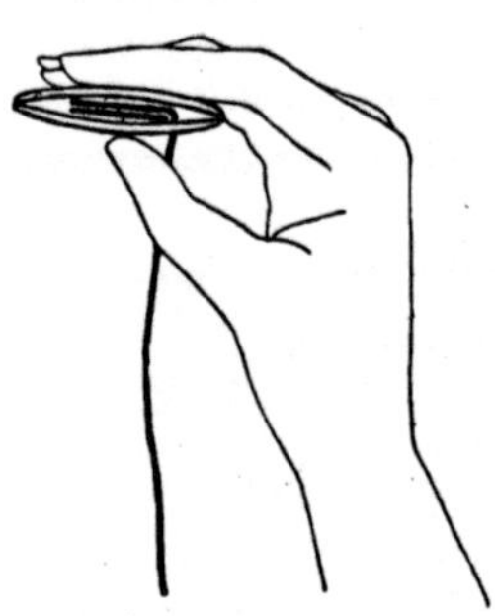

Fig. 37.

What to do with the Left Hand

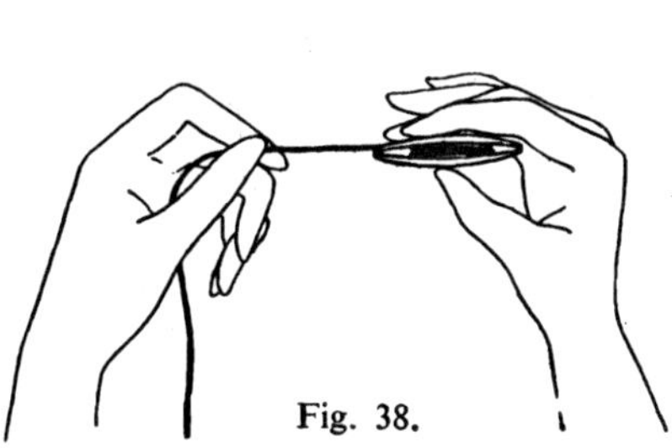

Fig. 38.

STEP 4. Grasp the free end of the thread between the thumb and forefinger (Fig. 38).

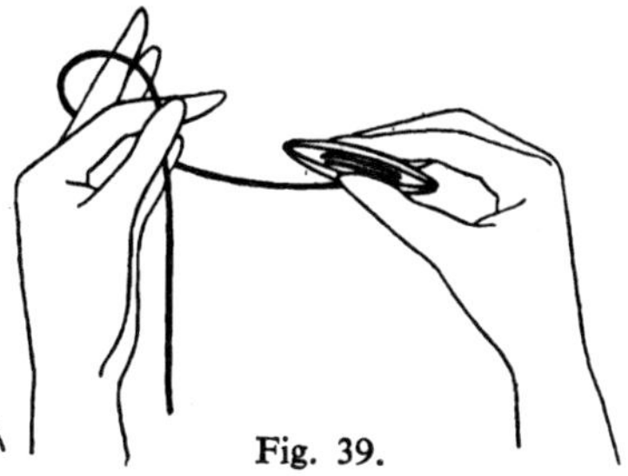

Fig. 39.

STEP 5. Spread out the middle, ring and little fingers and pass the thread over them (Fig. 39).

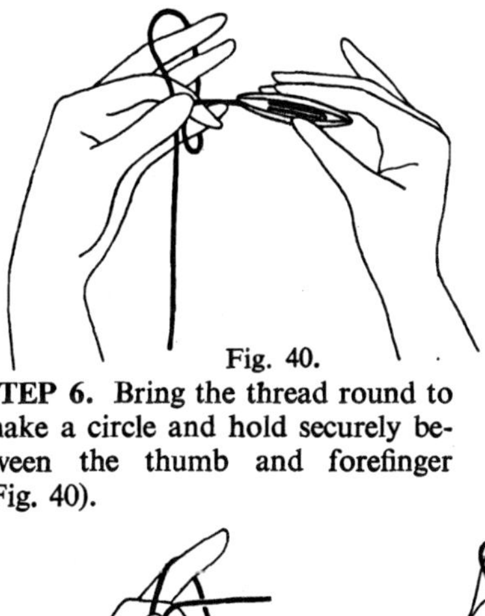

Fig. 40.

STEP 6. Bring the thread round to make a circle and hold securely between the thumb and forefinger (Fig. 40).

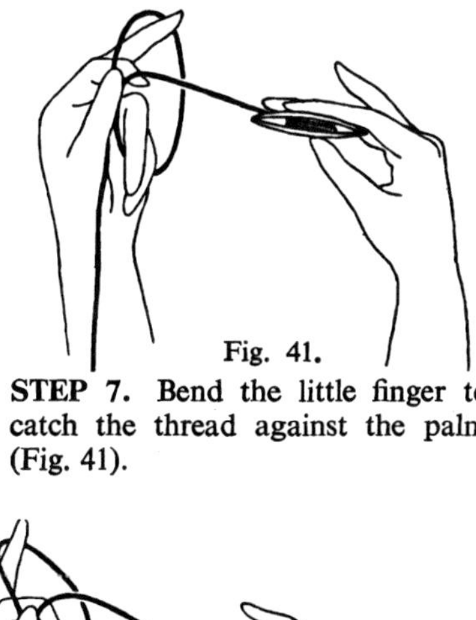

Fig. 41.

STEP 7. Bend the little finger to catch the thread against the palm (Fig. 41).

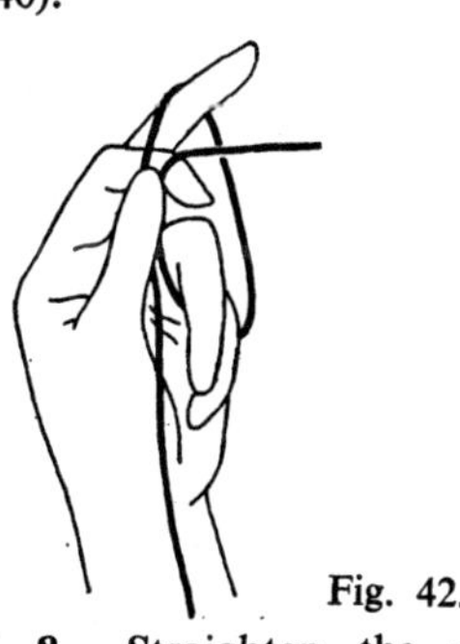

Fig. 42.

STEP 8. Straighten the middle finger back to catch the loose part of the circle thread (Fig. 42).

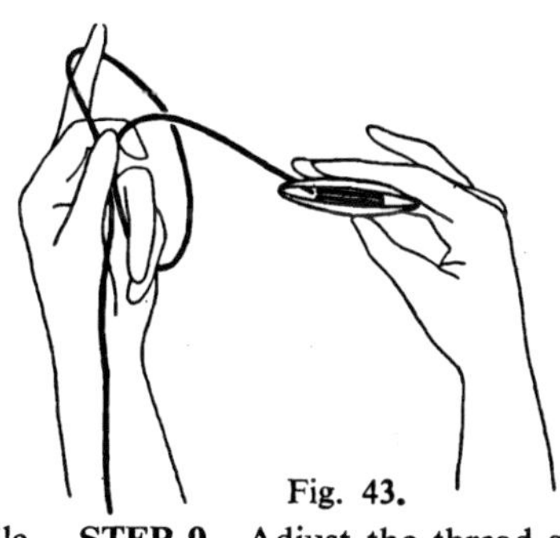

Fig. 43.

STEP 9. Adjust the thread so that the fingers do not feel strained (Fig. 43).

The Double Stitch (the basic stitch)

FIRST HALF OF DOUBLE STITCH

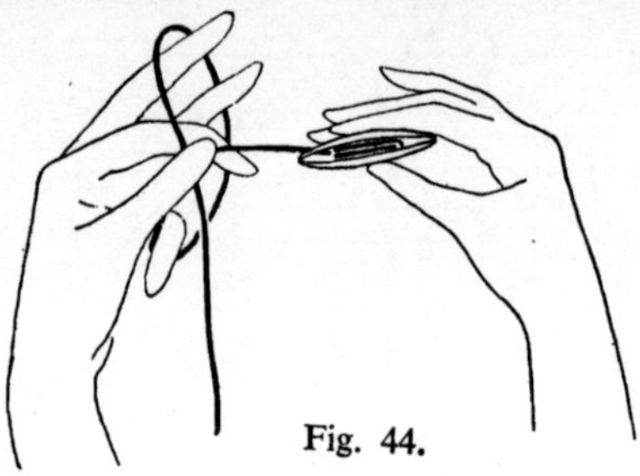

Fig. 44.

STEP 10. Draw shuttle thread out to its full length keeping right and left hands at equal levels (Fig. 44).

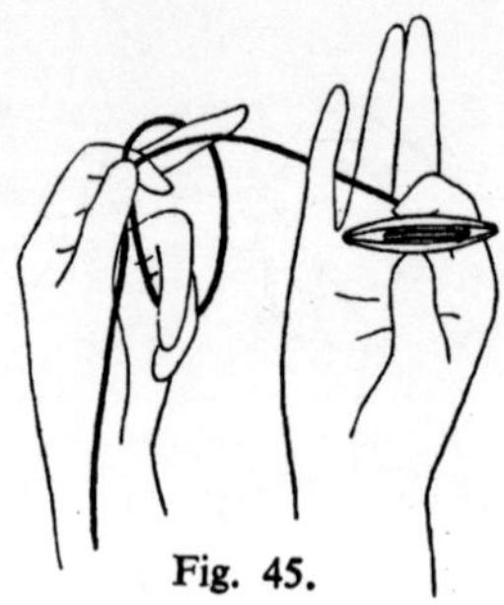

Fig. 45.

STEP 11. Pass the shuttle thread under the fingers then over the little finger of right hand (Fig. 45).

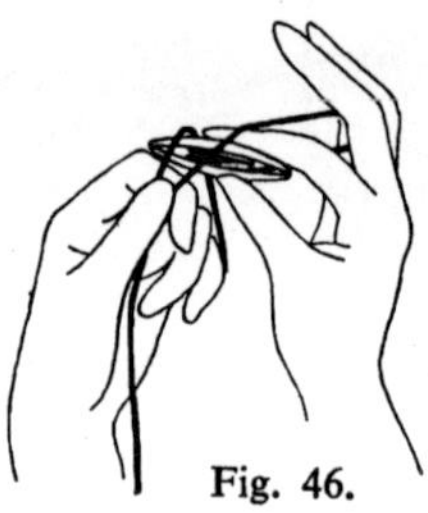

Fig. 46.

STEP 12. With thread in this position, drop middle finger of left hand and move the shuttle forward and insert it **under** both threads (Fig. 46)

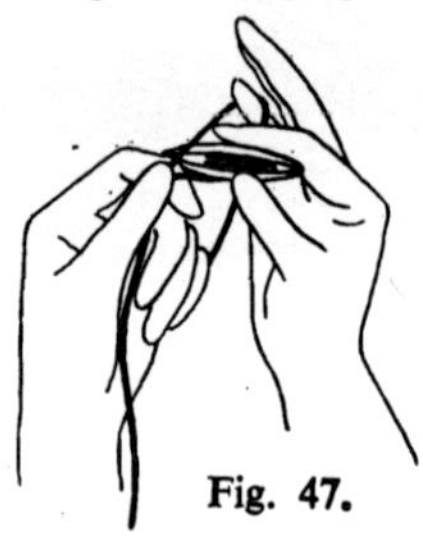

Fig. 47.

and bring it back **over** the thread held between thumb and forefinger of left hand and under shuttle thread (Fig. 47).

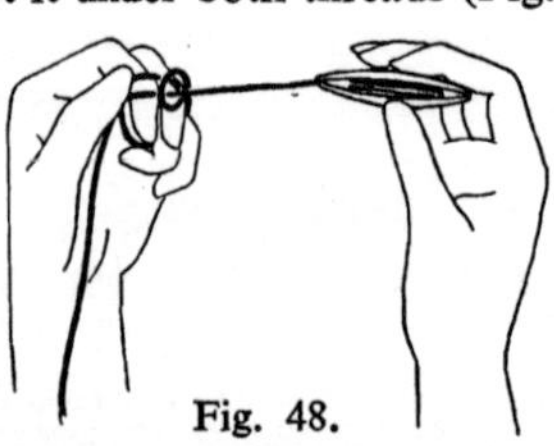

Fig. 48.

STEP 13. Drop thread from little finger of right hand and **draw shuttle thread taut** (Fig. 48), pass shuttle thread over little finger as before and hold in this position until first half of the double stitch is completed.

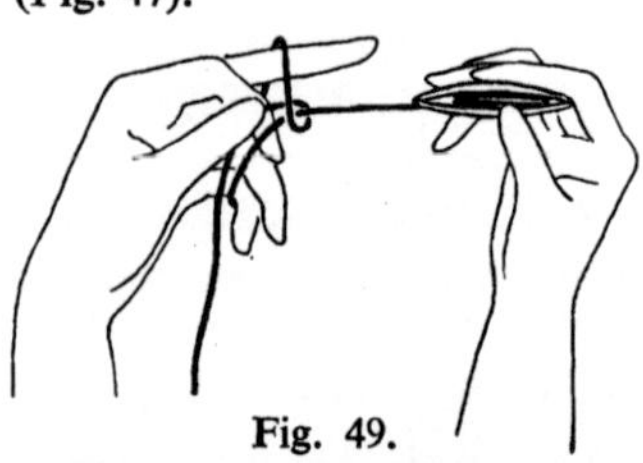

Fig. 49.

STEP 14. Slowly raise middle finger of left hand, thus sliding loop into position between thumb and forefinger (Fig. 49). This completes first half of **double stitch.**

NOTE. Before proceeding with Step 15, may we point out that it is important to relax the fingers of the left hand when drawing the shuttle thread tight as in Step 13. This allows the loop formed in Step 12 to turn from shuttle thread and be made by the thread round fingers of left hand. The shuttle thread passes through the loop now made.

SECOND HALF OF DOUBLE STITCH

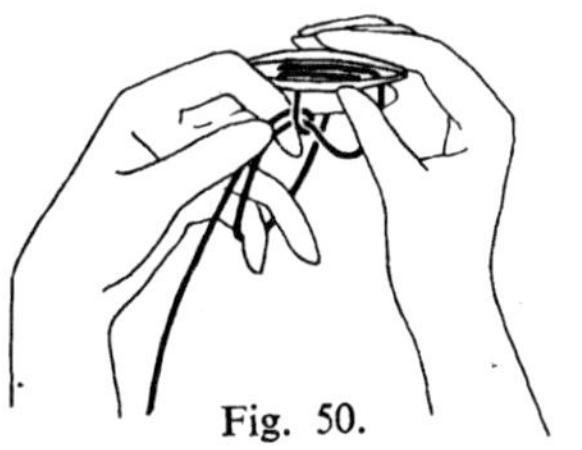

Fig. 50.

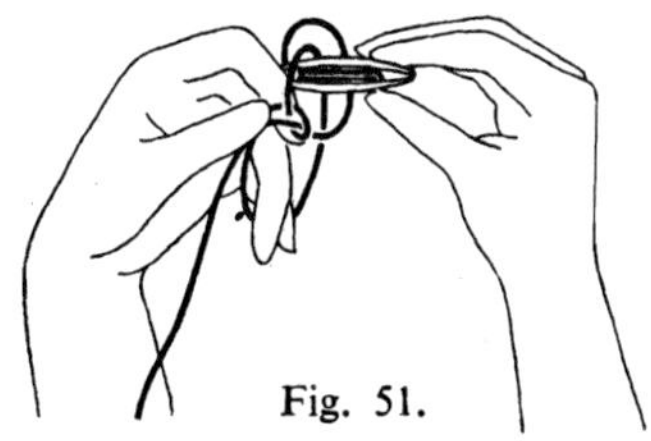

Fig. 51.

STEP 15. Drop thread from little finger of right hand. Move shuttle forward again and keeping pointed end of shuttle towards you, carry it **over** and bring it back **under** the thread held between thumb and fore-finger of left hand (Figs. 50 and 51).

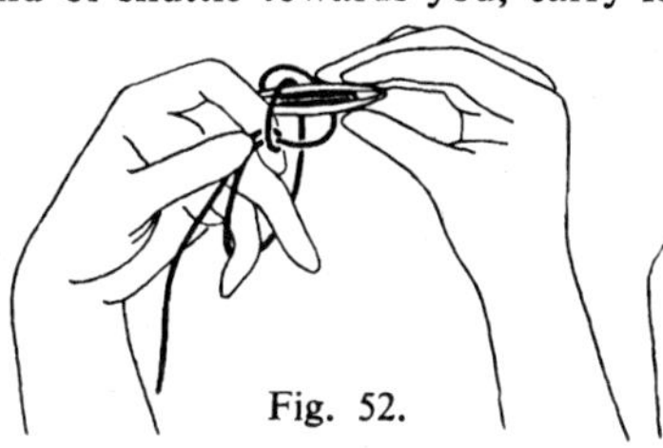

Fig. 52.

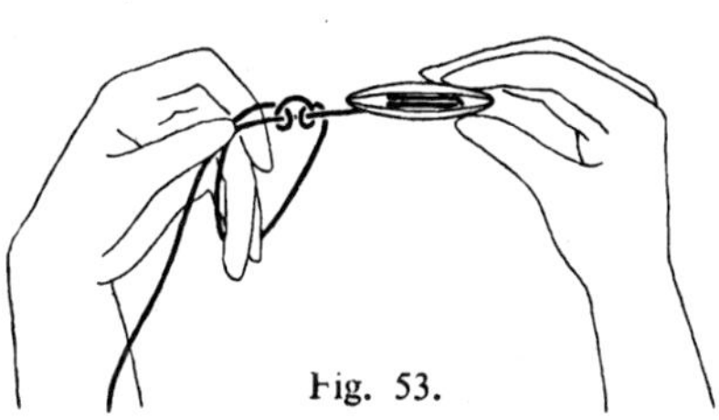

Fig. 53.

STEP 16. Drop middle finger of left hand.

STEP 17. Draw shuttle thread taut and hold in this position until second half of the double stitch is completed.

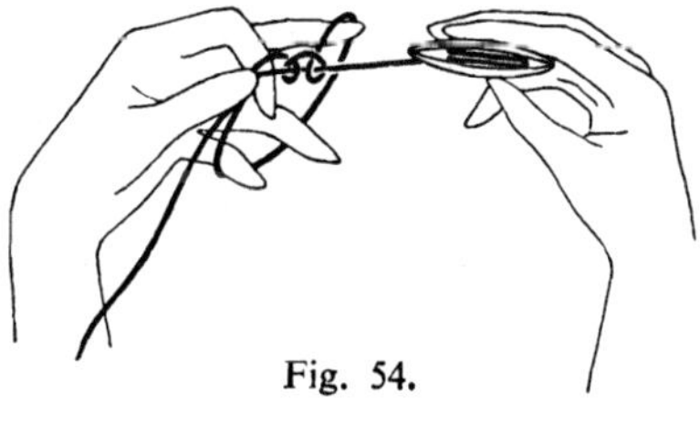

Fig. 54.

STEP 18. Slowly raise middle finger, thus sliding loop into position between thumb and forefinger of left hand (Fig. 54). This completes second half of Double Stitch, the basic stitch in Tatting.

FOR LEFT-HANDED PUPILS

The directions for each stitch apply to both **right- and left-handed** pupils. **Left-handed** pupils work from **left to right**. Place a pocket mirror to the left of each illustration and you will see the exact position in which you work reflected in the mirror.

Rings, Picots and Joinings

All tatting designs contain rings and picots. The rings form the basis of the design. The picots are used for decoration and for joining. Practice the following directions. They give in detail the fundamentals of rings, picots and joinings. When your rings are even and your picots uniform in size, cut off your practice piece and begin to work your selected article.

First Ring

NOTE. The working stitch always comes between the thumb and forefinger. In Figs. 55, 56 and 57 the fingers should come where the arrow points. The drawings are made in this manner so that all the steps may be clear.

STEP 1. Make four double stitches (ds).

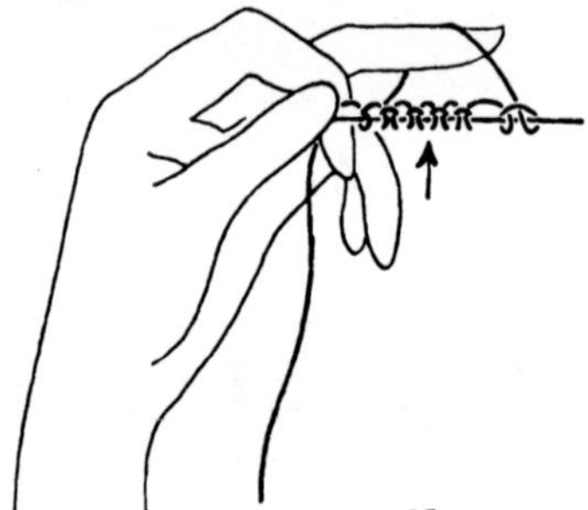

Fig. 55.

STEP 2. Next make the first half of a double stitch (ds), but as you slide it into position stop about $\frac{1}{4}$ in. from the preceding double stitch (ds) (Fig. 55).

STEP 3. Complete the double stitch (ds) (Fig. 56).

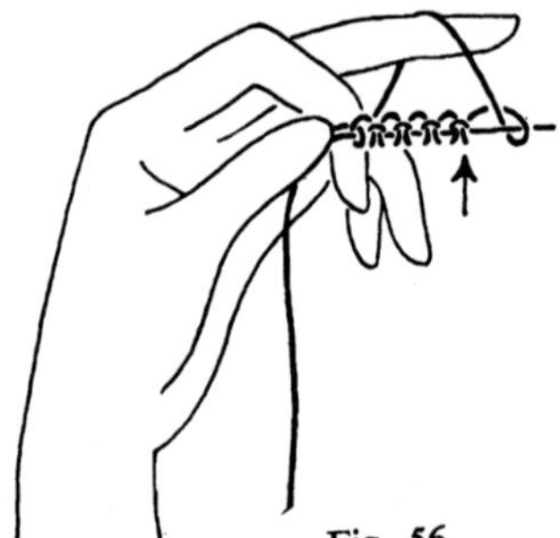

Fig. 56.

STEP 4. Draw the entire stitch close to the first four stitches (Fig. 57). The little loop formed from the space left between the stitches is a *picot* (p).

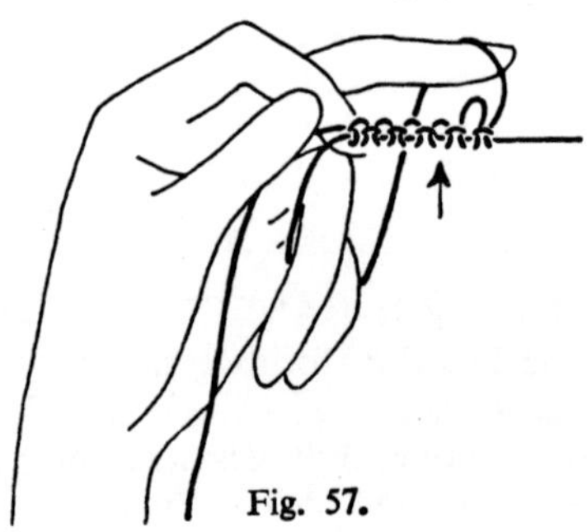

Fig. 57.

STEP 5. Make four more double stitches (ds).

STEP 6. Please note that steps 2, 3, 4 and 5 should be written 1 picot (p) and 5 double stitches (ds). A picot refers only to the loop and does not include the double stitch which fastens the loop.

STEP 7. Make another picot and five double stitches (see Step 6).

STEP 8. Make a picot and four double stitches.

Fig. 58.

STEP 9. Holding the stitches securely between thumb and forefinger of left hand, draw the shuttle thread tight so that the first and last stitches meet, forming a ring (Fig. 58).

Second Ring and Joinings

STEP 1. Wind the thread round the left hand in position for another ring.

STEP 2. Make 4 double stitches (ds) $\frac{1}{4}$ in. away from ring just made.

STEP 3. Insert hooked end of a crochet hook through the last picot of previous ring and catch the thread encircling left hand.

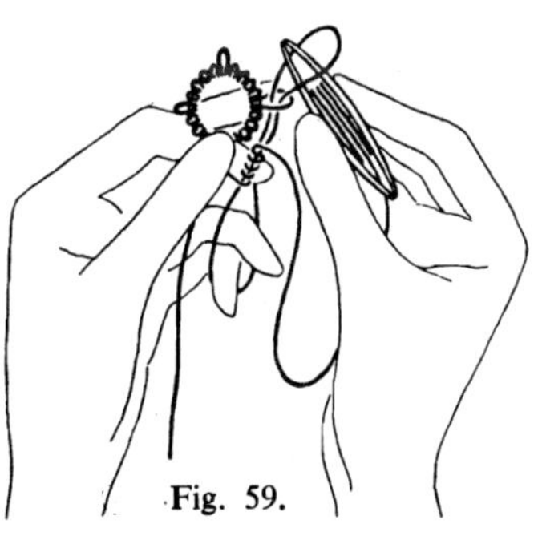

Fig. 59.

STEP 4. Pull the thread through until there is a loop large enough to insert shuttle (Fig. 59).

STEP 5. Pull the shuttle through loop and draw the shuttle thread tight.

STEP 6. Slowly raise middle finger of left hand to draw up the loop. This joins the new ring to the old one and counts as the first half of the next double stitch.

STEP 7. Complete the double stitch.

STEP 8. Repeat Steps 5 to 9 under *First Ring*.
Continue in this manner for each succeeding ring, repeating Steps 1 to 8 under *Second Ring and Joinings*.

Edging for handkerchief No. 1

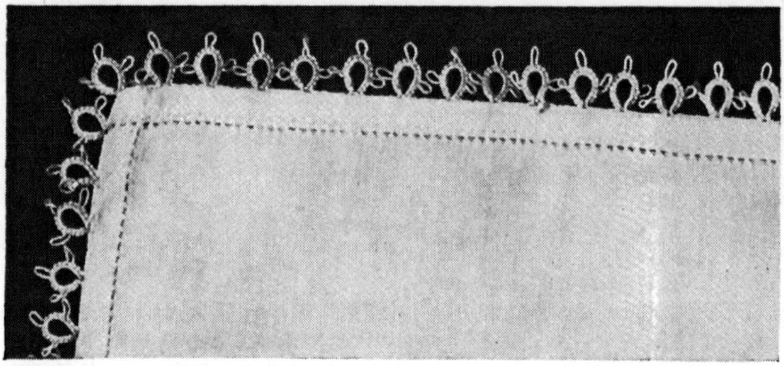

The preceding directions have been given in detail so as to make the steps clear in your mind. Now you are ready to read the same directions as they would appear in a book. (The abbreviations are explained to make the directions easier for a beginner to read.)

EDGING No. 1

R (ring) of 4 ds (double stitches), 3 p's (picots), sep (separated) by 5 ds, 4 ds, cl (close), * sp (space) of $\frac{1}{4}$ in., r (ring) of 4 ds, 3 p's sep by 5 ds, 4 ds, cl; repeat from * for length required.
Sew to handkerchief.

ABBREVIATIONS USED IN TATTING

R	ring
lr	large ring
sr	small ring
ds	double stitch
p	picot
lp	long picot
smp	small picot
sep	separated
cl	close
rw	reverse work
sp	space
ch	chain

JOINING THE THREAD

When a new thread is required make a flat knot close to the base of the last ring or chain, but do not cut off the ends, for the strain of the work may loosen the knot. If you make a knot in the thread, cut it off and tie the new thread close to last ring. Knots prevent the ring from being drawn up, for they will not pass through the double stitches. Cut off loose ends later.

REVERSING

In tatting you will have noticed that the rounded end of the loop on which you are working faces the top. However, you can produce an effect such as that shown in Handkerchief Edging No. 2 by turning your work first up and then down. The directions will say rw (reverse work). To do this, the ring you have just worked is

Edging for handkerchief No. 2

turned so that the base of the ring faces the top and the new ring is worked as usual with the loop side up.

EDGING No. 2

* R of 5 ds, p, 5 ds, cl. Rw, sp ($\frac{1}{8}$ in.). R of 4 ds, 3 p's sep by 4 ds, 4 ds, cl. Rw, sp ($\frac{1}{8}$ in.), 1 r of 5 ds, join to p of first r, 2 ds, 5 p's sep by 2 ds, 5 ds, cl. Rw and make another r like second, joining to 3rd p of second r. Rw and make another r like first, joining to last p of 3rd r. Rw and make another r like second, joining to adjacent r. Rw, sp; repeat from * for length required, joining to first p of 1 r.

USING BALL THREAD, AND SHUTTLE

Some tatting designs contain chains besides rings and picots. Rings can be made only with the shuttle thread wound in a complete circle round the left hand. Chains can be made only with a thread wound halfway round the hand (Fig. 60). When rings and chains appear in the same design it is necessary to use two working threads (a shuttle thread and a ball thread). Tie end of ball thread to end of shuttle thread.

When you are making a ring use the shuttle thread in the usual way.

When the ring is completed and you wish to make a chain, turn it so that the base of the ring is held between the thumb and forefinger (see Fig. 60). Stretch the ball thread over the back of the fingers in same way as shuttle thread, but instead of making a complete circle, wind it round the little finger to control tension (see Fig. 60). Work over the ball thread

(*continued on page 57*)

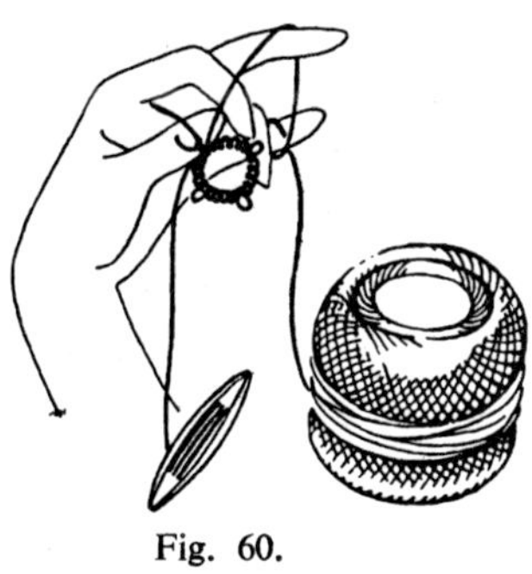

Fig. 60.

HANKIE EDGING No. 1, *see page 54*

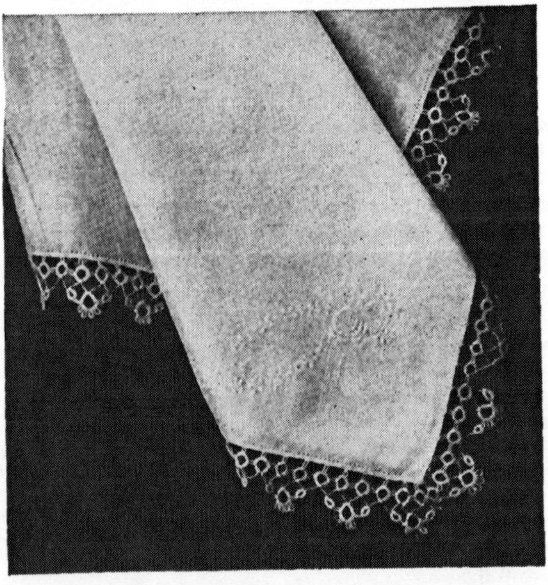

HANKIE EDGING No. 2, *see page 55*

Two Shuttles

When you wish to work rings in two colours, two shuttles are used. The two colours (one in each shuttle) may be alternated. When this takes place you drop the shuttle which made the preceding ring, pick up the second shuttle and make a ring as before. When the rings are separated by a chain, hold the thread of the second shuttle like the ball in Fig. 60.

Long Picot

To make a long picot, make a longer space between double stitches.

Josephine knot

This is an ornamental ring, consisting of the first half of a double stitch made a specified number of times.

---

continued from page 55

with the shuttle in the same manner as in making rings. (Picots and joinings are made in the same way as on rings.) When you have finished the chain, pull the stitches close together and put down the ball thread. Pick up the shuttle thread to make another ring.

Tatted Edgings

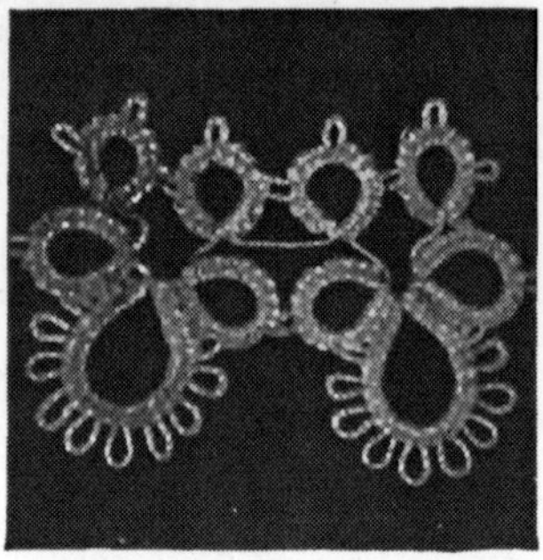

Materials in all instances. Mercer-Crochet No. 60 or No. 70 (20 gram). 1 ball selected colour. Tatting shuttle.

No. 1

Sr of 4 ds, 3 smp's sep by 4 ds, 4 ds, cl. Rw, sp of $\frac{1}{8}$ in., r of 9 ds, smp, 4 ds, smp, 5 ds, cl. * R of 5 ds, join to last smp of preceding r, 2 ds, 8 p's sep by 2 ds, 2 ds, smp, 5 ds, cl. R of 5 ds, join to smp of preceding r, 4 ds, smp, 9 ds, cl (last 3 r's constitute a clover). Rw, sp of $\frac{1}{8}$ in., r of 4 ds, join to last smp of last sr, (4 ds, smp) twice, 4 ds, cl. Sp of $\frac{3}{8}$ in., sr of 4 ds, join to last smp of preceding r, (4 ds, smp) twice, 4 ds, cl. Rw, sp of $\frac{1}{8}$ in., r of 9 ds, join to smp of last r of clover, 4 ds, smp, 5 ds, cl; repeat from * for length required. Fasten off.

No. 2

1st Row. Tie ball and shuttle threads together. Sr of 4 ds, 3 smp's sep by 4 ds, 4 ds, cl. * Rw, ch of 5 ds, p, 5ds. Rw, lr of 4 ds, join to last smp of preceding r, 6 ds, p, 6 ds, smp, 4 ds, cl. Rw, ch of 5 ds, p, 5 ds. Rw, sr of 4 ds, join to smp of preceding r, 4 ds, 2 smp's sep by 4 ds, 4 ds, cl; repeat from * for length desired, ending with a sr. Tie and cut.

2nd Row. Fasten ball and shuttle threads to 2nd p of first r of first row. Ch of 2 ds, smp, 9 ds, p, 9 ds, smp, 2 ds, * miss 1 r, join free p of next sr of first row. Ch of 2 ds, join to last p of preceding ch, 9 ds, p, 9 ds, smp, 2 ds; repeat from * to end. Tie and cut.

6

5

4

3

2

1

EDGINGS Nos. 1 to 6

Tatted Edgings

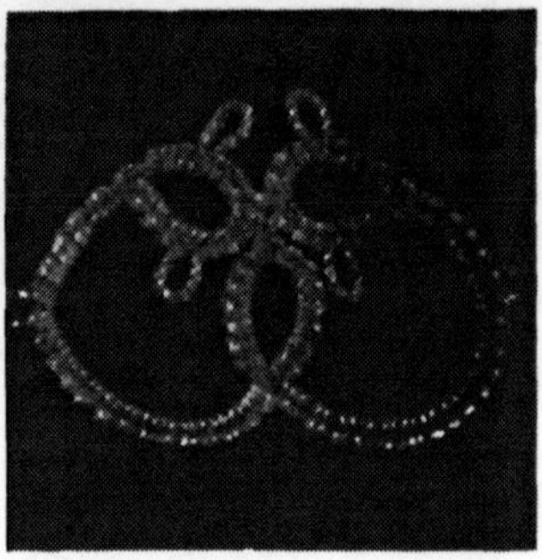

No. 3

1st Row. Tie ball and shuttle threads together. R of 6 ds, smp, 5 ds, smp, 1 ds, cl. * R of 1 ds, join to smp of preceding r, (5 ds, smp) twice, 1 ds, cl. R of 1 ds, join to smp of preceding r, 5 ds, smp, 6 ds, cl (shamrock made). Rw, ch of 16 ds. Rw, r of 6 ds, join to smp of preceding r, 5 ds, smp, 1 ds, cl; repeat from * for length required. Tie and cut.

2nd Row. Fasten ball and shuttle threads to sp at base of first shamrock of first row. Ch of 2 ds, smp, * 4 ds, 7 p's sep by 2 ds, 4 ds, smp, 2 ds, join to sp at base of next shamrock. Ch of 2 ds, join to last smp of preceding ch; repeat from * to end of row. Tie and cut.

No. 4

Tie ball and shuttle threads together. R of 4 ds, 3 p's sep by 4 ds, 4 ds, cl. Rw, ch of 6 ds, smp, 14 ds. * Rw, r of 8 ds, join to 2nd p of preceding r, 8 ds, cl. Rw, ch of 14 ds, smp, 6 ds. Rw, r of 4 ds, p, 4 ds, join to 2nd p of next to last r, 4 ds, p, 4 ds, cl. Ch of 4 ds, p, 4 ds. R of 4 ds, 3 p's sep by 4 ds, 4 ds, cl. Rw, ch of 6 ds, join to smp of next to last ch, 14 ds; repeat from * for length required, ending with rw, r of 4 ds, p, 4 ds, join to 2nd p of next to last r, 4 ds, p, 4 ds, cl. Tie and cut.

Tatted Edgings

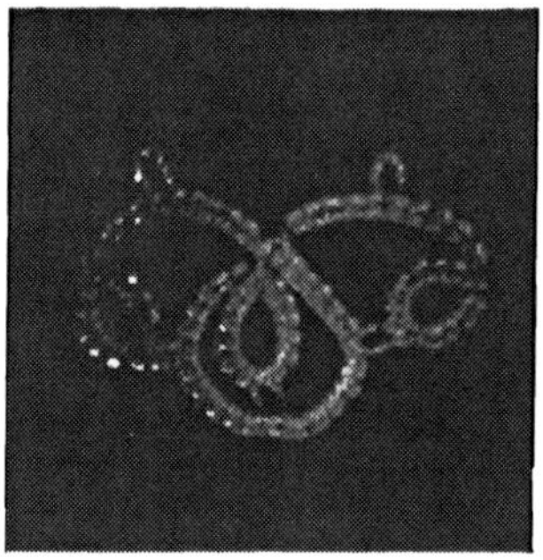

No. 5

Tie ball and shuttle threads together. Lr of 4 ds, smp, 4 ds, p, 4 ds, smp, 4 ds, cl. * Rw. ch of 3 ds, p, 7 ds, smp, 1 ds. Rw, sr of 1 ds, 9 smp's sep by 1 ds, 1 ds, cl. Ch of 6 ds, join to last smp of last lr, 4 ds, miss 1 p on last sr, join to next p, (ch of 10 ds, miss next p on same sr, join to next p) three times. Ch of 4 ds, smp, 6 ds, join to base of sr (flower made). Rw, ch of 1 ds, join to smp on adjoining ch, 7 ds, p, 3 ds. Rw, lr of 4 ds, join to smp of last ch of flower, 4 ds, p, 4 ds, smp, 4 ds, cl; repeat from * for length required. Tie and cut.

No. 6

Tie ball and shuttle threads together. * Sr of 6 ds, smp, 6 ds, cl. Rw, ch of 5 ds, p, 6 ds. Rw, lr of 7 ds, smp, 7 ds, cl. Ch of 6 ds, join to smp of sr, 6 ds, join to smp of lr, 6 ds, smp, 6 ds and fasten ball thread to sp at base of lr. Rw, ch of 6 ds, p, 5 ds. Rw, sr of 6 ds, join to smp in next to last ch, 6 ds, cl. Rw, sr of 6 ds, smp, 6 ds, cl. Rw, ch of 6 ds, p, 6 ds. Rw, r of 6 ds, join to smp of preceding r, 6 ds, cl. Rw; repeat from * for length required. Tie and cut.

Doily

This is a very simple edging introducing you to two rows, the first row being composed entirely of rings and the second row with rings and chains joining to rings of first row. When finished it is mounted on to a circular piece of linen, thus making a simple but very effective doily.

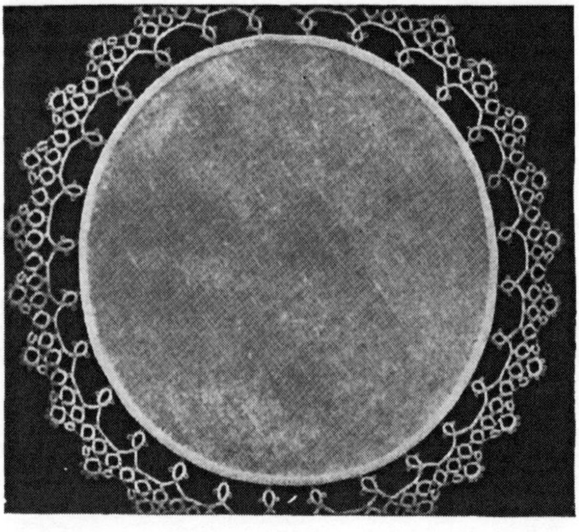

bright as a jewel on the dining table

Materials. Mercer-Crochet No. 20 (20 gram). 1 ball selected colour. Tatting shuttle. Piece of linen, 8 in. square.

Completed doily measures about 9½ in. in diameter.

Cut circle of linen 8 in. in diameter and hem.

EDGING

1st Row. With shuttle thread make a r of 4 ds, 3 p's sep by 4 ds, 4 ds, cl (first ring). * Rw, sp (⅛ in.), r of 4 ds, p, 4 ds, cl, rw, sp, r of 4 ds, join to last p of adjacent r, 4 ds, p, 4 ds, p, 4 ds, cl (2nd ring). Rw, sp, r of 4 ds, join to p of adjacent r, 2 ds, 5 p's sep by 2 ds, 4 ds, cl. Rw, sp, r of 4 ds, join to last p of adjacent r, 4 ds, p, 4 ds, p, 4 ds, cl (3rd ring). Rw, sp, r of 4 ds, join to last p of adjacent r, 4 ds, cl, rw, sp, r of 4 ds, join to last p of adjacent r, 4 ds, p, 4 ds, p, 4 ds, cl.

Repeat from * until piece measures 26 in. making edging into a circle by joining 3rd ring to the first p on first ring made, rw, sp, r of 4 ds, join to last p of adjacent r, 4 ds, cl. Tie and cut.

Tie shuttle and ball threads together.

2nd Row. * R of 4 ds, 3 p's sep by 4 ds, 4 ds, cl. Rw, make a ch of 5 ds, join to centre p of 3rd ring of first row, 5 ds, join to centre p of 2nd ring of first row, 5 ds, join to centre p of first ring of first row, 5 ds. Let ball hang, rw, and repeat from * all round. Join to base of first r of 2nd row. Tie and cut.

Sew to linen.

Collar (petals)

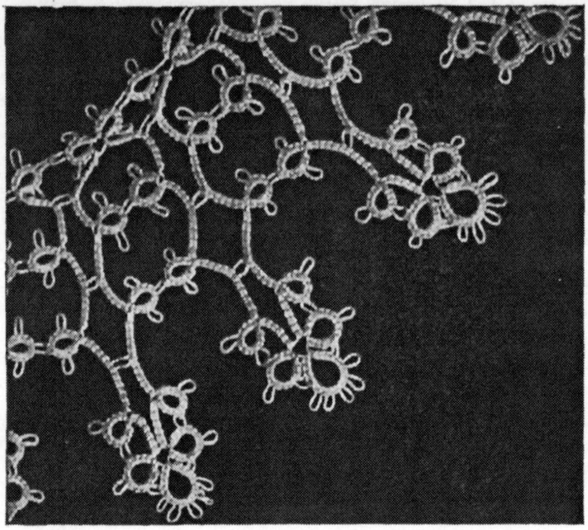

Rings and chains worked down from neck to edge and from edge to neck are all that is necessary to make this pretty petaled collar. Cuffs could be made to match if so desired by simply making less repeats.

Materials. Mercer-Crochet No. 40 (20 gram). 1 ball selected colour. Tatting shuttle.

R of 3 ds, 3 p's sep by 3 ds, 3 ds, cl. Close to this make r of 3 ds, 3 p's sep by 3 ds, 3 ds, cl. (Rw, ch of 6 ds, p, 6 ds, rw, r of 3 ds, 3 p's sep by 3 ds, 3 ds, cl) twice. * Rw, ch of 6 ds, p, 6 ds, rw, r of 4 ds, p, 4 ds, p, 4 ds, cl. Rw, ch of 6 ds, rw, r of 4 ds, join to p of adjacent r, 4 ds, p, 4 ds, p, 4 ds, cl. R of 4 ds, join to p of adjacent r, 2 ds, 6 p's sep by 2 ds, 4 ds, cl. R of 4 ds, join to last p of previous r, 4 ds, p, 4 ds, p, 4 ds, cl. Rw, ch of 6 ds, rw, r of 4 ds, join to p of adjacent r, 4 ds, p, 4 ds, cl. (Rw, ch of 6 ds, join to p of opposite ch, 6 ds, rw, r of 3 ds, 3 p's sep by 3 ds, 3 ds, cl) twice. Rw, ch of 6 ds, join to p of opposite ch, 6 ds, r of 3 ds, p, 3 ds, join to centre p of adjacent r, 3 ds, p, 3 ds, cl. R of 3 ds, 3 p's sep by 3 ds, 3 ds, cl, ch of 6 ds, p, 6 ds, rw, r of 3 ds, p, 3 ds, join to centre p of opposite r, 3 ds, p, 3 ds, cl, rw, ch of 6 ds, p, 6 ds, rw, r of 3 ds, p, 3 ds, join to centre p of opposite r, 3 ds, p, 3 ds, cl; repeat from * for length required for collar, making end to correspond with beginning. Tie and cut.

REFRESHMENT SET (*see next page*)

Refreshment Set

(*See previous page*)

Now we come to the motifs system, where small motifs are made and joined together to form mats. Here we have a large doily and six small ones, but chair-backs, runners or guest towels' edgings could easily be made from this small motif design.

Materials. Mercer-Crochet No. 20 (20 gram). 3 balls selected colour. Tatting shuttle.
This material is sufficient to make a large doily about 8 in. square and 6 glass doilies each about 4½ in. square.

GLASS DOILY (make 6)
Tie ball and shuttle threads together.

FIRST MOTIF
R of 7 ds, smp, 3 ds, smp, 7 ds, cl. Rw, ch of 5 ds, 3 p's sep by 5 ds, 5 ds. * Rw, r of 7 ds, join to adjacent p of previous r, 3 ds, smp, 7 ds, cl. Rw, ch of 5 ds, 3 p's sep by 5 ds, 5 ds; repeat from * once more, rw, r of 7 ds, join to p of previous r, 3 ds, join to first p of first r, 7 ds, cl. Rw, ch of 5 ds, 3 p's sep by 5 ds, 5 ds, join to base of first r. Tie and cut.

SECOND MOTIF
Work as for first motif, joining the 3rd p of one ch and the first p of following ch of second motif to corresponding p's on 2 ch's of first motif. Tie and cut.
Make 4×4 motifs, joining to adjacent motifs as second motif was joined to first, leaving centre p free on corner chains of each motif.

LARGE DOILY
Make 7×7 motifs, joining as for glass doilies.

Cheval set

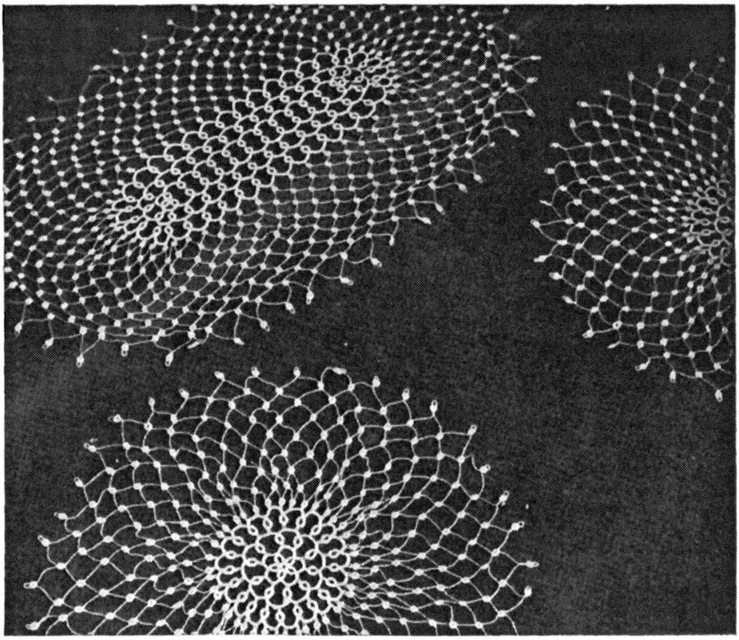

A superb example of Tatting with all its lacy refinement.

(*See overleaf*)

Cheval set

(*See photo on previous page*)

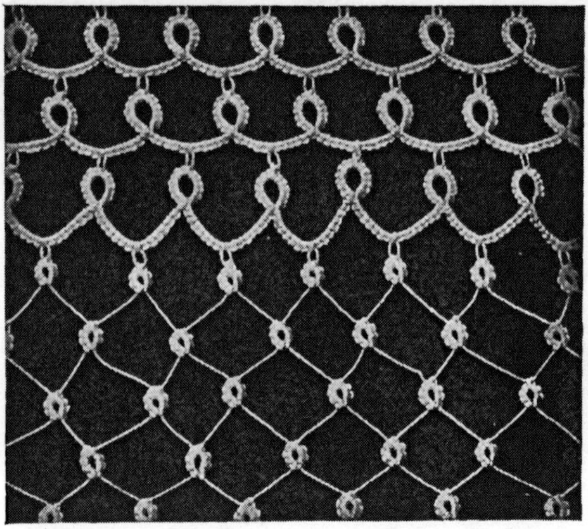

This looks more complicated than it really is. After working the first three rows of rings and chains it is only a matter of making rings with spaces between, which get longer as the doily grows.

Materials. Mercer-Crochet No. 40 (20 gram). 1 ball selected colour. Tatting shuttle.

MEASUREMENTS

Round Doily—11 in. in diameter.
Oval Doily—10 in. × 16 in.

Round Doily (Make 2)

STAR

Tie ball and shuttle threads together, r of 8 ds, 1 p, 8 ds, cl. * Rw, ch of 4 ds, p, 6 ds, p, 4 ds. Rw, r of 8 ds, join to 1 p of first r, 8 ds, cl; repeat from * 3 times more. Rw, ch of 4 ds, p, 6 ds, p, 4 ds. Join to base of first r. Tie and cut.

1st Row. R of 8 ds, join to any p of star, 8 ds, cl. * Rw, ch of 4 ds, 1 p, 6 ds, 1 p, 4 ds. Rw, r of 8 ds, join to next p on star, 8 ds, cl; repeat from * joining last ch to base of first r. Tie and cut.

2nd Row. As first row, joining to 1 p of first row.

3rd Row. R of 4 ds, join to any p on previous row, 4 ds, cl. * Sp of $\frac{3}{4}$ in., r of 4 ds, join to next p on previous row, 4 ds, cl; repeat from * to end of row. Hereafter mark the end of each row.

4th Row. * Sp of $\frac{3}{4}$ in., r of 4 ds, join to thread between next 2 r's on previous row, 4 ds, cl; repeat from * to end of row.

5th to 9th Row. Work same as 4th row, only making the sp between r's $\frac{1}{4}$ in. longer.

10th Row. * Sp of $\frac{3}{4}$ in., r of 4 ds, p, 4 ds, cl, sp of $\frac{3}{4}$ in., r of 4 ds, join to sp between next 2 r's on previous row, 4 ds, cl; repeat from * ending with sp of $\frac{3}{4}$ in., r of 4 ds, p, 4 ds, cl, sp of $\frac{3}{4}$ in., join to r of previous row. Tie and cut.

Oval Doily

1st Row. R of 8 ds, 1 p, 8 ds, cl. * Rw, ch of (4 ds, p) twice, 4 ds. Rw, r of 8 ds, join to 1 p of first r, 8 ds, cl; repeat from * once more—end made. Work long side as follows: ** Rw, ch of 6 ds, p, 6 ds. Rw, r of 8 ds, p, 8 ds, cl; repeat from ** nine times more. Rw, ch of 6 ds, p, 6 ds. Make other end as follows: Rw, r of 8 ds, 1 p, 8 ds, cl. (Rw, ch of 4 ds, p, 4 ds, p, 4 ds, rw, r of 8 ds, join to 1 p of this end r, 8 ds, cl) twice. Work along opposite side as follows: Rw, ch of 6 ds, p, 6 ds. Rw, r of 8 ds, join to corresponding p on long side of oval, 8 ds, cl. Continue thus across, joining last ch to base of first r. Tie and cut.

2nd Row. R of 8 ds, join to first p on first ch of previous row, 8 ds, cl. Rw, ch of (4 ds, p) twice, 4 ds. Rw, r of 8 ds, join to next p on same ch, 8 ds, cl. Rw, ch of (4 ds, p) twice, 4 ds. Rw, r of 8 ds, join to first p on next ch, 8 ds, cl. Rw, ch of (4 ds, p) twice, 4 ds. Rw, r of 8 ds, join to next p on same ch, 8 ds, cl—end completed. * Rw, ch of 6 ds, p, 6 ds. Rw, r of 8 ds, join to p on next ch, 8 ds, cl; repeat from * across to opposite end. Work other end and opposite side to correspond, joining last ch to base of first r. Tie and cut.

3rd Row. R of 8 ds, join to p on last ch of previous row, 8 ds, cl. * Rw, ch of (6 ds, p) twice, 6 ds. Rw, r of 8 ds, join to free p, 8 ds, cl; repeat from * six times more—end completed. ** Rw, ch of 8 ds, p, 8 ds. Rw, r of 8 ds, join to next p on previous row, 8 ds, cl; repeat from ** across. Then work other end and opposite side to correspond, joining last ch to base of first r. Tie and cut.

4th Row. As 3rd row of round doily.

5th to 12th Row. As 4th row of round doily.

13th Row. As 10th row of round doily. Starch and press.

TATTING * page 70

Luncheon set

(*See photographs opposite*)

Now we come to a little more advanced kind of design, but do not hesitate on that account as it is soon mastered and the effort is worth while as you will find out.

Mounted on to linen to match your china it would give you a very lovely table setting.

Materials. Mercer-Crochet No. 20 (20 gram). 3 balls of selected colour. Tatting shuttle. $1\frac{1}{8}$ yd. of linen, 36 in. wide.

Above material is sufficient for a luncheon set consisting of a centre mat about 14 in. × 36 in. and 4 place mats about 12 in. × 18 in. Edging measures 2 in. wide.

Centre Mat

Cut linen $14\frac{1}{2}$ in. × $32\frac{1}{2}$ in. Make a narrow hem all round. Use shuttle and ball thread.

1st Row. Tie shuttle and ball threads together. Make a r of 4 ds, p, 3 ds, 3 p's sep by 2 ds, 3 ds, p, 4 ds, cl. Rw, make another ring the same. Rw, ch of 9 ds, rw, make a clover as follows: R of 4 ds, join to last p of adjacent r, 3 ds, 3 p's sep by 2 ds, 3 ds, p, 4 ds, cl. Lr of 4 ds, join to last p of last r, 3 ds, 5 p's sep by 2 ds, 3 ds, p, 4 ds, cl. R of 4 ds, join to last p of last lr, 3 ds, 3 p's sep by 2 ds, 3 ds, p, 4 ds, cl (the last 3 r's form clover). * Rw, ch of 9 ds, r of 4 ds, p, 3 ds, p, 2 ds, join to centre p of adjacent r, 2 ds, p, 3 ds, p, 4 ds, cl. Rw, r of 4 ds, join to last p of adjacent r, 3 ds, 3 p's sep by 2 ds, 3 ds, p, 4 ds, cl. Ch of 5 ds, rw, r of 4 ds, join to last p of adjacent r, 3 ds, 3 p's sep by 2 ds, 3 ds, p, 4 ds, cl. Rw, r of 4 ds, join to last p of adjacent r, 3 ds, 3 p's sep by 2 ds, 3 ds, p, 4 ds, cl. Ch of 9 ds, rw, make a clover as before. Rw, ch of 9 ds, r of 4 ds, p, 3 ds, p, 2 ds, join to centre p of adjacent r, 2 ds, p, 3 ds, p, 4 ds, cl. Rw, r of 4 ds, join to last p of adjacent r, 3 ds, 3 p's sep by 2 ds, 3 ds, p, 4 ds, cl. Rw, ch of 5 ds, rw, r of 4 ds, join to last p of adjacent r, 3 ds, 3 p's sep by 2 ds, 3 ds, p, 4 ds, cl. Rw, r of 4 ds, join to last p of adjacent r, 3 ds, 3 p's sep by 2 ds, 3 ds, p, 4 ds, cl. Rw, ch of 9 ds, rw, make a clover; repeat from * until work measures the length of one short side of centre mat. Tie ends and cut. Tie threads to 2nd p of lr of clover.

2nd Row. * Ch of 3 ds, p, 3 ds, miss one p, join to next p, ch of 3 ds, 6 p's sep by 3 ds, 3 ds, rw, r of 5 ds, p, 5 ds, join to centre p of next r of clover, 5 ds, p, 5 ds, cl. Rw, ch of 4 ds, rw, r of 6 ds, p, 5 ds, join in same place where 2 r's of first row are joined (below clover), 5 ds, p, 6 ds, cl. Rw, ch of 4 ds, rw, r of 5 ds, p, 5 ds, join to centre p of first r of next clover, 5 ds, p, 5 ds, cl. Rw, ch of 3 ds, join to last p of adjacent ch, ch of 3 ds, 5 p's sep by 3 ds, 3 ds, miss one p of lr of same

LUNCHEON SET

Luncheon Set *(continued from page 70)*

clover, join to next p; repeat from * across. Tie ends and cut. Sew to short side of centre mat. Finish other side in same way.

Place Mats (Make 4)

Cut 4 pieces of material, each 12½ in. × 15 in., and complete as for centre mat.

Collar No. 2

(*See opposite page*)

Introduces you to a more frilly type of article, but is no more difficult to do than the others. Rings and chains are all that is required to make this collar; work first the centre band then the top and bottom ruffles to complete collar.

Materials. Mercer-Crochet No. 20 (20 gram). 1 ball selected colour. Tatting shuttle.
Use shuttle and ball of thread.
Starting at neckline work neckband as follows:
With shuttle make a r of 4 ds, 3 p's sep by 4 ds, 4 ds, cl. Rw, sp (¼ in.), r of 4 ds, 3 p's sep by 4 ds, 4 ds, cl. * Rw, sp (¼ in.), r of 4 ds, join to corresponding p of adjacent r, 4 ds, p, 4 ds, p, 4 ds, cl; repeat from * across until piece measures 15 in. (or length required). Tie and cut.

TOP RUFFLE

Tie ball and shuttle threads together.
1st Row. R of 4 ds, p, 4 ds, join to 2nd (centre) p of first r of neckband, 4 ds, p, 4 ds, cl. * Rw, ch of 5 ds, p, 5 ds, rw, r of 4 ds, p, 4 ds, join to free p of next r of neckband, 4 ds, p, 4 ds, cl; repeat from * across, ending with a ring.
2nd Row. * Ch of 3 ds, 5 p's sep by 3 ds, 3 ds, rw, r of 4 ds, p, 4 ds, join to p of adjacent ch, 4 ds, p, 4 ds, cl, rw; repeat from * across, joining last ch to base of first r of first row. Tie and cut.

BOTTOM RUFFLE

1st Row. R of 4 ds, p, 4 ds, join to 2nd (centre) p of first r of neckband, 4 ds, p, 4 ds, cl. * Rw, ch of 3 ds, p, 3 ds, rw, r of 4 ds, p, 4 ds, join to free p of next r of neckband, 4 ds, p, 4 ds, cl; repeat from * ending with a ring.

2nd Row. Ch of 3 ds, p, 3 ds, * r of 4 ds, 3 p's sep by 4 ds, 4 ds, cl, rw, ch of 5 ds, join to p of adjacent ch, 5 ds, rw; repeat from * ending with one ring after last joining.

3rd Row. Rw, ch of 3 ds, 5 p's sep by 3 ds, 3 ds, * rw, r of 4 ds, p, 4 ds, join to centre p of adjacent r, 4 ds, p, 4 ds, cl. Rw, ch of 3 ds, 3 p's sep by 2 ds, 3 ds; repeat from * ending with ch of 3 ds, 5 p's sep by 3 ds, 3 ds, join to base of first r of previous row. Tie and cut.

4th Row. R of 4 ds, p, 4 ds, join to centre p of 3-p ch, 4 ds, p, 4 ds, cl. * Rw, ch of 3 ds, 4 p's sep by 2 ds, 3 ds. Rw, r of 4 ds, p, 4 ds, join to centre p of next ch, 4 ds, p, 4 ds, cl; repeat from * ending with a ring. Tie and cut.

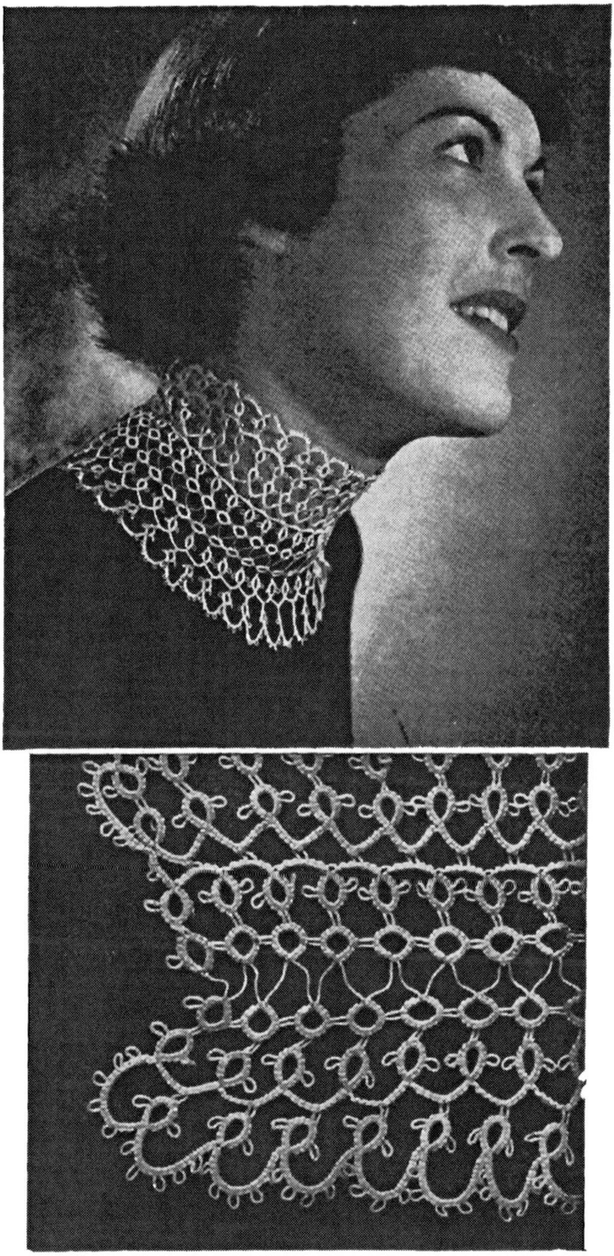

COLLAR No. 2

Handkerchief Edgings

These are also a little more complicated in design, but with a little practice you should be able to work them. Worked in No. 60 or 70 they should make a very dainty finish to your handkerchiefs.

Materials. Mercer-Crochet No. 60 (20 gram). 1 ball selected colour. Tatting shuttle.

No. 1

1st Row. Sr of 4 ds, p, 4 ds, p, 4 ds, cl. * Rw, ch of 4 ds, p, 4 ds, p, 4 ds. Rw, r of 4 ds, join to 2nd p of sr, 4 ds, p, 4 ds, p, 4 ds, cl. R of 4 ds, join to last p of preceding r, 4 ds, p, 4 ds, p, 4 ds, cl. Make one more r same as this, joining to preceding r as 2nd r was joined to first. Rw, ch of 4 ds, p, 4 ds, p, 4 ds. Rw, sr of 4 ds, join to last p of preceding r, 4 ds, p, 4 ds, cl; repeat from * for length desired. At corners, make the ch's that precede and follow the 3 r group of 4 ds, p and 4 ds. Tie and cut.

2nd Row. Attach thread to free p of first r, ch of 3 ds, p, 3 ds, * join to joining p of first and 2nd r, ch of 4 ds, 4 p's sep by 4 ds, 4 ds. Join to joining p of 2nd and 3rd r's. Ch of 3 ds, p, 3 ds, join to free p of last r of 3 r group and free p of r on next 3 r group. Ch of 3 ds, p, 3 ds; repeat from * across. Sew to edge of handkerchief.

HANDKERCHIEF EDGINGS

No. 2 No. 1

No. 2

Handkerchief Edgings, *continued*

No. 2 (*See previous page*)

CORNER MOTIF

Starting at one of the 2 centre rings, make a r of 8 ds, p, 6 ds, p, 8 ds, cl. Rw, ch of 8 ds, p, 8 ds, p, 8 ds. Rw, r of 8 ds, join to 2nd p of preceding r, 6 ds, p, 8 ds, cl. Rw, ch of 6 ds. Rw, r of 8 ds, p, 6 ds, p, 6 ds, p, 8 ds, cl. R of 8 ds, join to last p of preceding r, 6 ds, p, 6 ds, p, 8 ds, cl. Make one more r same as this, joining to the preceding r as before. Rw, ch of 6 ds. Rw, r of 8 ds, join to last p of preceding r, 6 ds, p, 8 ds, cl. Rw, ch of 6 ds. Rw, r of 8 ds, p, 8 ds, p, 8 ds, cl. Rw, sr of 6 ds, join to free p of 2nd r, 6 ds, cl. Rw, r of 8 ds, join to 2nd p of adjacent r, 8 ds, p, 8 ds, cl. Rw, ch of 9 ds. Rw, r of 8 ds, p, 8 ds, p, 8 ds, cl. Rw, sr of 6 ds, join to free p on first r, 6 ds, cl. Rw, r of 8 ds, join to 2nd p of adjacent r, 8 ds, p, 8 ds, cl. Rw and work remainder of motifs to correspond, join last ch of 6 ds to first r. Tie and cut.

OUTER ROW

Attach ball thread to free p on centre r of 3 r group and make ch of 6 ds, p, 6 ds, p, 6 ds, join to adjacent r that has one free p, make one more ch same as this, join to free p of next r, make one more ch as before, join to joining p of 2 r's, make centre ch of 6 ds, 3 p's sep by 6 ds, 6 ds, join to joining p of next 2 r's and complete r to correspond with beginning. Tie and cut. Cut off one corner of handkerchief (about ¾ in. from point of corner) and hem. Sew lace corner to linen.

EDGING

1st Row. Fasten thread to edge of handkerchief, * ch of 5 ds, p, 2 ds, p, 2 ds, p, 5 ds, join to handkerchief, leaving ⅜ in. space; repeat from * along entire edge. Tie and cut.

2nd Row. Attach thread to first p of first r, * ch of 4 ds, p, 4 ds, join to 3rd p of same scallop, ch of 2 ds, join to first p of next scallop; repeat from * all around. Tie and cut.

Mat

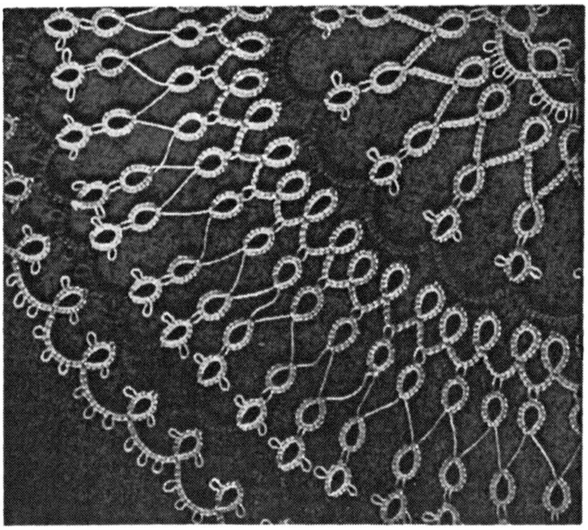

Here we introduce you to working with two colours at the same time. The rings are made with selected colour and the chains between in a contrasting colour. There is nothing difficult about it and it is worth while when finished.

Materials. Mercer-Crochet No. 20 (20 gram). 1 ball selected colour. 1 ball each of two contrasting colours. Tatting shuttle.

Measurement. 11 in. in diameter.

With selected colour, tie ball and shuttle threads together.

1st Row. R of 4 ds, 3 p's sep by 4 ds, 4 ds, cl. Rw, * ch of 3 ds, 4 p's sep by 2 ds, 3 ds, rw, r of 4 ds, join to last p of previous r, 4 ds, 2 p's sep by 4 ds, 4 ds, cl, rw; repeat from * 8 times more, joining last p of last r to first p of first r, ch of 3 ds, 4 p's sep by 2 ds, 3 ds, join to base of first r. Tie and cut.

2nd Row. Tie ball and shuttle threads together. R of 8 ds, join to first p of first ch of first row, 8 ds, cl, * rw, ch of 7 ds, r of 8 ds, p, 8 ds, cl, ch of 7 ds, rw, r of 8 ds, miss one p, join to next p of same ch, 8 ds, cl, rw, ch of 7 ds, r of 8 ds, p, 8 ds, cl. Ch of 7 ds, rw, r of 8 ds, join to first p of next ch of first row, 8 ds, cl; repeat from * ending with rw, ch of 7 ds, r of 8 ds, p, 8 ds, cl, ch of 7 ds, join to base of first r. Tie and cut.

3rd Row. With selected colour in shuttle and one of the contrasting balls tie threads together. * R of 4 ds, p, 4 ds, join to p of r of second row, 4 ds, p, 4 ds, cl. Rw, ch of

4 ds, 3 p's sep by 4 ds, 4 ds, rw; repeat from * joining last ch to base of first r. Tie and cut.

4th Row. With selected colour in both shuttle and ball tie threads together. * R of 8 ds, join to p of ch of previous row, 8 ds, cl, rw, ch of 4 ds, p, 4 ds, rw; repeat from * joining last ch to base of first r. Tie and cut.

5th Row. With selected colour in shuttle. * R of 8 ds, join to p of ch of previous row, 8 ds, cl, rw, sp of $\frac{1}{2}$ in., r of 8 ds, p, 8 ds, cl, rw, sp of $\frac{1}{2}$ in.; repeat from *, join to base of first r. Tie and cut.

6th Row. With selected colour in shuttle and other contrasting colour on ball tie threads together. * R of 4 ds, p, 4 ds, join to p of r of previous row, 4 ds, p, 4 ds, cl, rw, ch of 3 ds, 3 p's sep by 3 ds, 3 ds, rw; repeat from * joining last ch to base of first r. Tie and cut.

7th Row. With selected colour in shuttle and ball tie threads together. * R of 4 ds, p, 4 ds, join to centre p of ch of previous row, 4 ds, p, 4 ds, cl, rw, ch of 3 ds, 3 p's sep by 3 ds, 3 ds, rw; repeat from * joining last ch to base of first r. Tie and cut.

☆ TENERIFFE LACE ☆

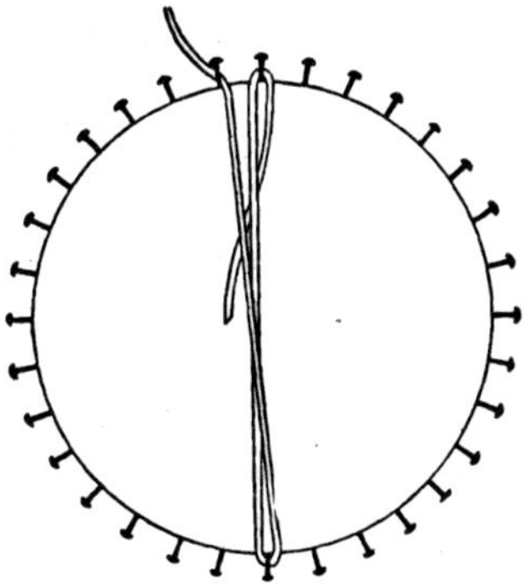

1. Begin to wind the thread round the pins in this way.

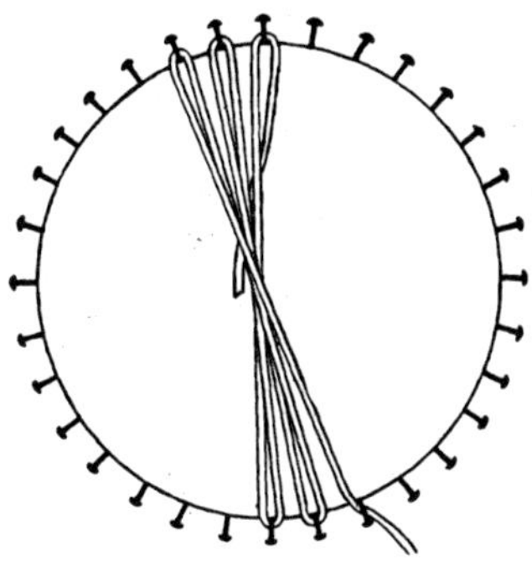

2. This shows how to wind the thread round the second pair of pins.

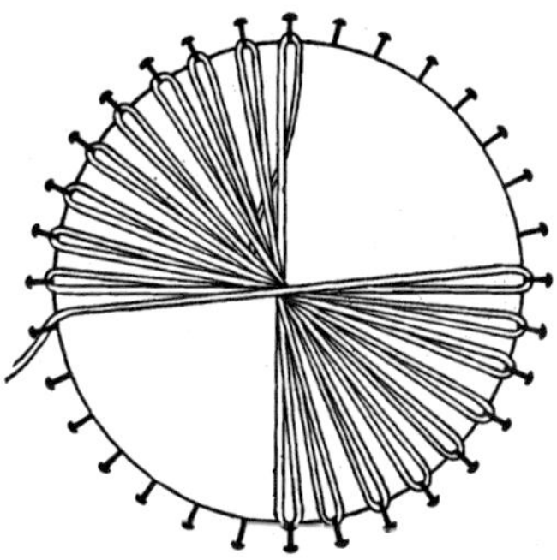

3. The work should look like this when the disc is partly full.

4. The centre of the motif is darned and a round of knotting is being worked.

In this, simple lace motifs join together to make delightful table mats, edgings, insertions, etc. Begin by making a circle of cardboard 2 or 3 in. in diameter, according to the size preferred. Into the thickness of the cardboard put 32 pins at regular intervals. One motif can be made on each side of the disc. Withdraw pins when motif is completed.

Any thickness of Mercer-Crochet can be used according to the article being made. For trimmings, the finer numbers are best and for mats use No. 5, 10, 15 or 20. Figs. 1, 2 and 3 show how the winding is done. Using ball thread complete winding. Break off leaving sufficient thread so that all the rest of the work can be done without having to join on another length. Thread this through the eye of a short, fairly thick, needle and take to the centre of the motif. Now darn the centre, working alternately over and under two of the foundation threads and drawing the thread to the centre so that it is very closely worked. (When finishing one row and commencing the other it will be necessary to work over or under four threads so as to be lifting the opposite threads on the next row.) Work three rows of darning then a row of knotting (see a row in process of being worked in Fig. 4). This centre is worked on all motifs, sometimes the knotting row is left out, but the darning is necessary to keep the threads in order.

Important. Mercer-Crochet should be used for best results. Purchase the necessary amount of thread at one time so that it is of the same dye lot number.

Washing Instructions. Use a warm lather of pure soap flakes and wash in the usual way. Pull into shape when drying and press with hot iron on wrong side. If the crochet requires to be slightly stiffened dip into a thin solution of starch, pin out on a clean board with rustless pins and leave to dry.

Maltese Pattern Motif

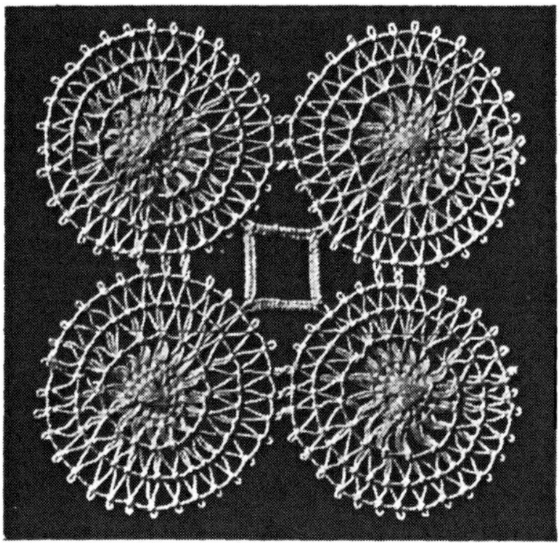

Work in the same way as given on left for the centre but without the first knotting round. Take the thread about $\frac{1}{4}$ in. above the darning and work a round of knotting taking four threads together. Now work another knotting round the same distance away, this time taking two threads at a time in same manner as Simple Wheel Motif. Work a final knotting round just below the pins. (*See illustration above.*)

TO MAKE UP MOTIFS

The motifs should be joined to each other by the picot loops. Join 3 picots of one motif to 3 picots of corresponding motif, leaving 5 picots free between joinings. A button stitch bar is worked in centre of 4 motifs, working over 2 threads laid from 3rd free picot of one motif to 3rd free picot on next motif.

Wheel Motif

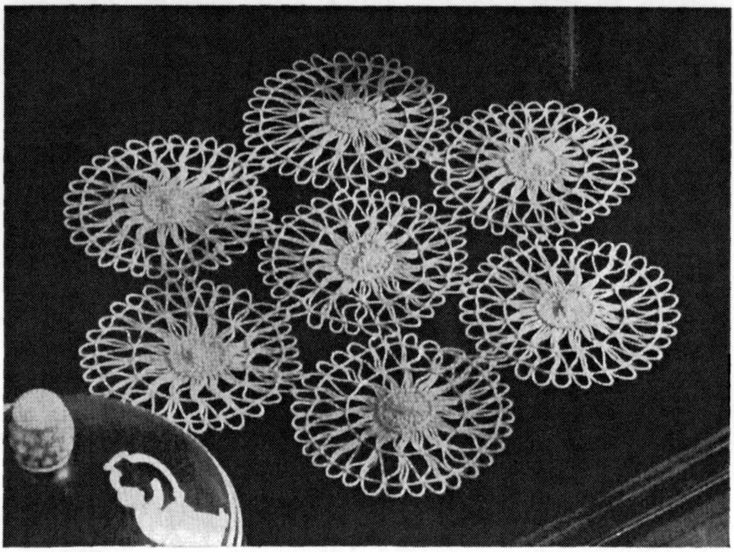

Work as explained until the centre is darned, then work a round of knotting over 2 threads. Take the thread halfway between this round and the edge and work another round of knotting over 4 threads, taking care to allow enough thread between the groups for motif to lie flat (Fig. 4, page 79).

Work another row of knotting, this time over two threads just below the pins, taking one thread from each group and two centre threads alternately. Fasten off. Join as shown in illustration.

☆ KNITTED LACE ☆

KNIT YOUR OWN household lace: edgings, mats, tablecloths, chair-backs, etc., are most attractive and long-lasting when knitted in Mercer-Crochet. This cotton is less elastic than wool, and in order to produce a satisfactory texture finer needles in proportion to the thickness of thread should be used.

Begin with a coarse number—No. 5 or 10—and remember to keep the working thread fairly tight.

A design which commences in the centre with a small number of stitches is constructed by casting on all the stitches on one needle and then dividing them evenly on to three or four needles as required for the pattern on the first round of knitting.

1. CASTING-ON

With 2 Needles

(*a*) Begin with a slip knot and put the needles into it as shown. * Pass the thread from the ball round and between the points of the needles (Fig. 61).

61

(*b*) With the right-hand needle pull through a loop (Fig. 62).

62

(*c*) Put this loop on to the left-hand needle, slip right-hand needle to back of left-hand needle and continue from * in this way for the number of stitches required (Fig. 63).

63

(*d*) This shows how to arrange the cast-on stitches for working in rounds (Fig. 64).

64

Thumb Method

(*e*) Leave an end of the thread and make a slip knot. Pass the end over

CASTING-ON

Thumb Method (*continued*)

the thumb as shown and knit into the loop thus made. Draw out the thumb and repeat for the number of stitches required (Fig. 65).

65

Invisible Cast-on

(*a*) This method of casting-on is used when no hard edge is required and when a fringe is to be added. Take a piece of thread and holding the two needles as shown wind the ball thread over and round these with the extra thread so that when one needle is withdrawn, the extra thread holds the loops and makes a foundation for the knitting (Fig. 66).

66

(*b*) The foundation thread is being taken out to leave loops for fringe (Fig. 67).

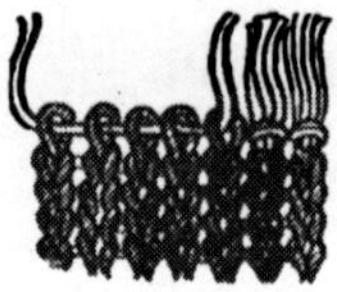

67

68

2. KNIT STITCH

The four stages of working a knot or plain stitch.

(*a*) Put the right-hand needle into the loop under the left-hand needle as shown (Fig. 68).

69

(*b*) Pass the thread round and between the points of the needles (Fig. 69).

(*c*) Pull a loop through on the point of the right-hand needle. This makes the new stitch. Now slip old stitch from left needle (Fig. 70).

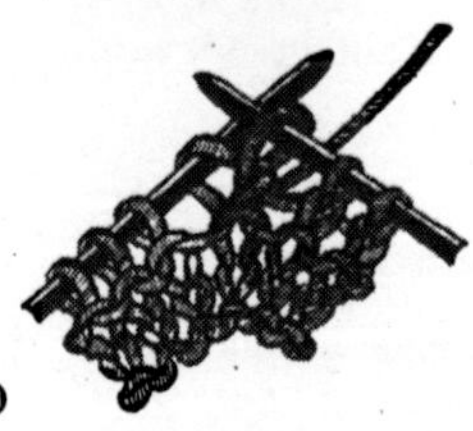

70

(*d*) The new stitch is complete and the right-hand needle is ready to be put into the next loop (Fig. 71).

71

3. PURL STITCH

Put the right-hand needle through the loop as shown. Pass the thread round the point of the needle and pull a loop through. Slip old stitch from left needle (Fig. 72).

72

4. DECREASING

The two most usual methods of decreasing.

(*a*) **Knit Two Together.** Put the right-hand needle through two loops and knit in the ordinary way (Fig. 73).

73

(*b*) **Pass Slip Stitch Over.** Put the right-hand needle into the loop on left-hand needle and slip stitch off. Knit next stitch. Put the point of the left-hand needle into the slipped stitch and lift it over the knitted stitch (Fig. 74).

74

(*c*) Movement completed (Fig. 75).

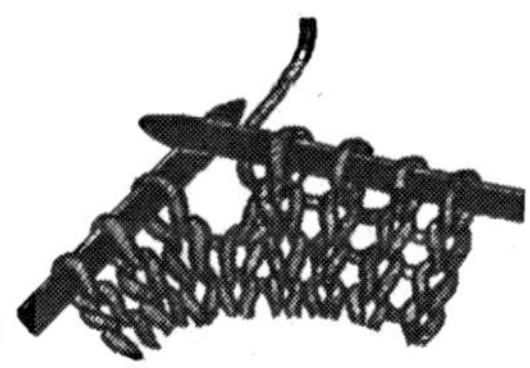
75

5. INCREASING

The four most usual ways of increasing.

(*a*) **Knit Twice in Stitch.** Knit into the stitch in the ordinary way and before dropping the loop off the needle, knit into back of it again and slip off needle (Fig. 76).

76

(*b*) **Pick Up Thread Between Stitches.** This shows the thread which has to be picked up, put back on the left-hand needle ready for knitting (Fig. 77).

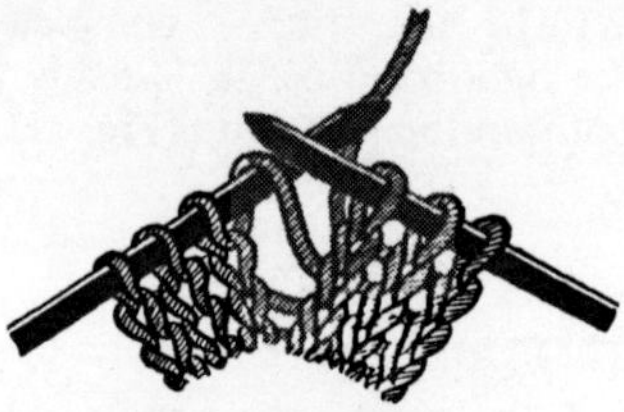

77

(*c*) **Knitting Into Stitch from Row Below.** The loop picked-up ready for putting on the left-hand needle for knitting (Fig. 78).

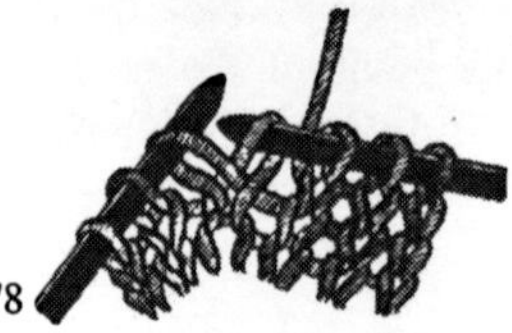

78

(*d*) **Pick Up Thread Between Stitches and Knit into Back of Loop.** The loop has been picked up and put on left-hand needle. The right-hand needle is put through the back of the stitch which twists it and prevents a hole being made (Fig. 79).

79

6. MATCHING INCREASINGS AND DECREASINGS

(*a*) The method of knitting twice into a stitch produces the effect of a horizontal bar in the knitting which automatically matches as shown here (Fig. 80).

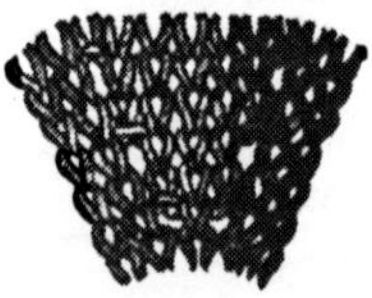

80

(*b*) To produce a matched effect when decreasing it is necessary to work 'slip one, knit one, pass the slipped stitch over' on the right and 'knit two together' on the left (Fig. 81).

81

7. 'MAKING' STITCHES FOR LACE PATTERNS

(*a*) **Thread Forward.** Bring the thread to the front of the work and knit the next stitch in the ordinary way (Fig. 82).

82

(*b*) **Thread Round Needle.** This is the same method as 7 (*a*) when worked between purl stitches (Fig. 83).

83

(*c*) **Thread Over Needle.** The same method when worked between a knit and a purl stitch (Fig. 84).

84

8. CASTING-OFF

(*a*) **Simple Casting-off.** Knit the first two stitches, then with the left-hand needle, lift the first loop over the second. Continue knitting a stitch and lifting the loop of the previous stitch over (Fig. 85).

85

(*b*) **Double Casting-off.** When the extra elastic edge is needed, cast-off twice in each stitch as shown. The stitch is knitted but the loop is left on the needle. The previous loop is then passed over the next one and the loop left on the needle is knitted. The previous loop is then passed over it in the ordinary way (Fig. 86).

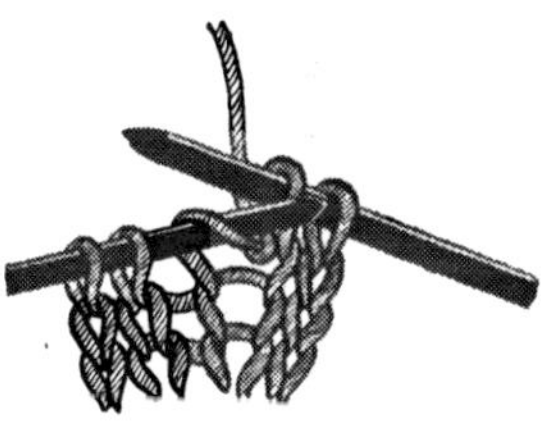

86

(*c*) **Crochet Casting-off.** For fine work some people use this method of finishing. As shown, each loop is hooked through the last (Fig. 87).

87

(*d*) **Invisible Casting-off.** To match the invisible cast-on edge, run a piece of thread through the last row of loops to hold them in position ready for the fringe to be added (Fig. 88).

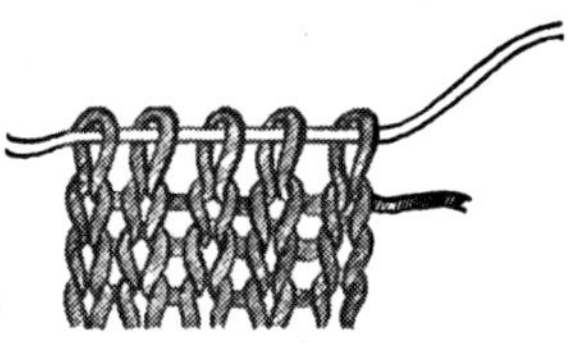

88

Knitted Lace Mat

HEXAGONAL MOTIFS

Materials. Mercer-Crochet No. 20 (20 gram). 2 balls selected colour. 1 set Milwards' Phantom Knitting Pins No. 14. 1 Milwards' Steel Crochet Hook No. 3.
Tension. One motif=5½ ins. from point to point.
Measurement. 15 ins. in diameter across centre.

MOTIF
Cast on 12 sts and divide evenly on 3 pins, k one round.

List of Abbreviations on p. 90

Pattern
1st Row. * K 1, th fwd, k 1; repeat from * to end of row.
2nd Row. * K 1, (k 1, p 1) into next st, k 1; repeat from * to end of row.
3rd Row. * Sl 1, k 1, p.s.s.o, th fwd, k 2 tog, th fwd; repeat from * to end of row.

4th Row. * K 1, (k 1, p 1) into next st, k 2; repeat from * to end of row.

5th Row. * Sl 1, k 1, p.s.s.o, th fwd, k 2 tog, th fwd, k 1, th fwd; repeat from * to end of row.

6th Row. * K 1, (k 1, p 1) into next st, k 4; repeat from * to end of row.

7th Row. * Sl 1, k 1, p.s.s.o, th fwd, k 2 tog, th fwd, k 3, th fwd; repeat from * to end of row.

8th Row. * K 1, (k 1, p 1) into next st, k 6; repeat from * to end of row.

9th Row. * Sl 1, k 1, p.s.s.o, th fwd, k 2 tog, th fwd, k 2 tog, k 1, sl 1, k 1, p.s.s.o, th fwd; repeat from * to end of row.

10th Row. As 8th row.

11th Row. * Sl 1, k 1, p.s.s.o, th fwd, k 2 tog, th fwd, k 5, th fwd; repeat from * to end of row.

12th Row. * K 1, (k 1, p 1) into next st, k 8; repeat from * to end of row.

13th Row. * Sl 1, k 1, p.s.s.o, th fwd, k 2 tog, th fwd, sl 1, k 1, p.s.s.o, k 3, k 2 tog, th fwd; repeat from * to end of row.

14th Row. As 12th row.

15th Row. * Sl 1, k 1, p.s.s.o, th fwd, k 2 tog, th fwd, k 7, th fwd; repeat from * to end of row.

16th Row. * K 1, (k 1, p 1) into next st, k 10; repeat from * to end of row.

17th Row. * Sl 1, k 1, p.s.s.o, th fwd, k 2 tog, th fwd, sl 1, k 1, p.s.s.o, k 5, k 2 tog, th fwd; repeat from * to end of row.

18th Row. As 16th row.

19th Row. * Sl 1, k 1, p.s.s.o, th fwd, k 2 tog, th fwd, sl 1, k 1, p.s.s.o, th fwd, k 5, th fwd, k 2 tog, th fwd; repeat from * to end of row.

20th Row. * K 1, (k 1, p 1) into next st, k 1, sl 1, k 1, p.s.s.o, th fwd, k 7, th fwd, k 2 tog; repeat from * to end of row.

21st Row. * Sl 1, k 1, p.s.s.o, th fwd, k 2 tog, th fwd, sl 1, k 1, p.s.s.o, k 1, sl 1, k 1, p.s.s.o, th fwd, k 1, th fwd, k 2 tog, k 1, k 2 tog, th fwd; repeat from * to end of row.

22nd Row. * K 1, (k 1, p 1) into next st, k 3, sl 1, k 1, p.s.s.o, th fwd, k 3, th fwd, k 2 tog, k 2; repeat from * to end of row.

23rd Row. * Sl 1, k 1, p.s.s.o, th fwd, k 2 tog, th fwd, k 1, sl 1, k 1, p.s.s.o, th fwd, k 5, th fwd, k 2 tog, k 1, th fwd; repeat from * to end of row.

24th Row. * K 1, (k 1, p 1) into next st, k 2, sl 1, k 1, p.s.s.o, th fwd, k 7, th fwd, k 2 tog, k 1; repeat from * to end of row.

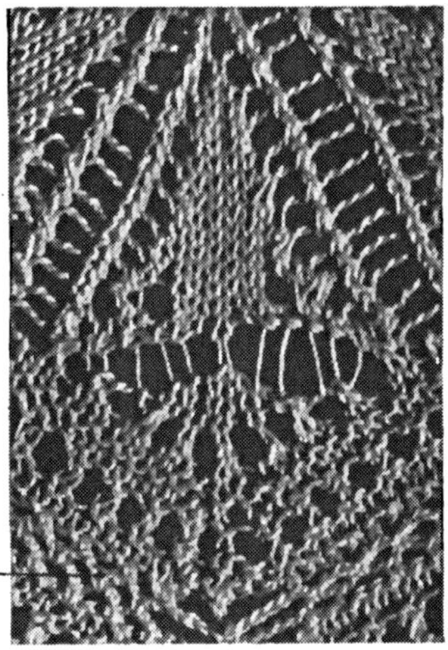

25th Row. * Sl 1, k 1, p.s.s.o, th fwd, k 2 tog, sl 1, k 1, p.s.s.o, th fwd, k 9, th fwd, k 2 tog; repeat from * to end of row.

26th Row. Before commencing this row, pass first st of each pin on to previous pin.

* (K 1, p 1) into next st, (k 2 tog, th fwd) twice, k 2 tog, (th fwd, k 1) 3 times, th fwd, (sl 1, k 1, p.s.s.o, th fwd) twice, sl 1, k 1, p.s.s.o; repeat from * to end of row.

27th Row. K.

28th Row. * K 9, (k 1, p 1) into next st, k 1, (k 1, p 1) into next st, k 7; repeat from * to end of row.

29th Row. P.

30th Row. * K 10, (k 1, p 1) into next st, k 1, (k 1, p 1) into next st, k 8; repeat from * to end of row.

31st Row. P.

32nd Row. (K 2 tog, th fwd) 6 times, * k 1, th fwd, (k 2 tog, th fwd) 11 times; repeat from * 4 times more, k 1, th fwd, (k 2 tog, th fwd) 5 times.

33rd Row. P.

34th Row. * K 11, (k 1, p 1) into next st, k 1, (k 1, p 1) into next st, k 10; repeat from * to end of row. Cast off purlwise.

Work 7 motifs in all.

To JOIN MOTIFS

It will be easier to lay all motifs on brown paper and pin in position, first 3 motifs in centre row, 2 above this row, arranging them so that they fit into each other, then place last 2 below centre row in same manner. Join thread on first st dividing holes past corner, * (3 ch, 1 dc) into the edge of one motif 10 times, spacing the dc to come above the sts dividing the row of holes in the knitting. Work 4 ch, 1 dbl tr into the extreme corner, then 4 ch, 1 dc into the next side of motif; repeat from * on each side of motif.

When working the edging on the second motif, work 1 ch, 1 dc into a loop on first motif, 1 ch, 1 dc into side of second motif. On the corners, after working first 4 ch, work 1 ss into the dbl tr on corner of first motif, 1 dbl tr into point of second motif, 4 ch, 1 dc into next side of second motif.

Work all *joining sides* of motif in this way and outside edges as first motif.

BORDER

1st Row. Join thread to a loop at junction of 2 motifs, (5 ch, 1 dc into next 3 ch loop) until last 3 ch loop on corner is reached, then work 6 ch, 1 dbl tr into dbl tr on corner of motif, (5 ch, 1 dbl tr into same place) twice, 6 ch, 1 dc into next 3 ch loop. Work second side in the same way, then down third side of motif to the last 3 ch loop. On the inner corners work 5 ch, 1 dc on to joining point of motifs, 5 ch, then work round all motifs to correspond with first, join with a ss to top of 5 ch loop at beginning of row.

2nd Row. * 6 ch, 1 dc into next loop; repeat from * until joining point of first motif is reached, 6 ch, 1 dc into 5 ch loop, 1 dc into next 5 ch loop (to link the two lower loops); repeat from first * all round motifs. Join with a dc into first loop.

3rd Row. * 3 ch, 1 ss into 3rd ch from hook, 1 dc into same loop as last dc, 3 ch, 1 ss into 3rd ch from hook, 1 dc into next loop; repeat from * to end of row, join with a ss. Fasten off.

Wash, starch and pin out to measurements.

KNITTING ABBREVIATIONS

K—knit; p—purl; st—stitch; sts—stitches; rep—repeat; th fwd—thread forward; tog—together; sl—slip; p.s.s.o.—pass slip stitch over; m st—moss stitch (k 1, p 1 alternately); ktb—k 2 tog through back; st st—stocking stitch; m 1—make 1 by thread forward on a knit row and thread round needle on a purl row; inc—increase; dec—decrease; patt—pattern.

Knitted Lace Tray Cloth

Materials. Mercer-Crochet No. 5 (20 gram). 3 balls white or ecru. 1 pair Milwards' Phantom Knitting Pins No. 14.

Tension. 9½ sts to 1 in. (approx.).

Measurements. Width 12 in. Length 19 in.

Cast on 113 sts and work in m st.

1st Row. K 1, * p 1, k 1. Rep from * to end. Repeat this row 9 times more. Continue in patt with m st borders thus:

1st Row. (K 1, p 1) 5 times, k 2, * m 1, sl 1, k 1, p.s.s.o, k 5, k 2 tog, m 1, k 1. Rep from * to last 11 sts, k 1, (p 1, k 1) 5 times.

2nd Row. (K 1, p 1) 5 times, p 3, * m 1, p 2 tog, p 3, p 2 tog, m 1, p 3. Rep from * to last 10 sts, (p 1, k 1) 5 times.

3rd Row. (K 1, p 1) 5 times, k 4, * m 1, sl 1, k 1, p.s.s.o, k 1, k 2 tog, m 1, k 5. Rep from * to last 19 sts, m 1, sl 1, k 1, p.s.s.o, k 1, k 2 tog, m 1, k 4, (p 1, k 1) 5 times.

4th Row. (K 1, p 1) 5 times, p 5, * m 1, p 3 tog, m 1, p 7. Rep from * to last 18 sts, m 1, p 3 tog, m 1, p 5, (p 1, k 1) 5 times.

5th Row. (K 1, p 1) 5 times, k 1, k 2 tog, * m 1, k 7, m 1, sl 1, k 2 tog, p.s.s.o. Rep from * to last 20 sts, m 1, k 7, m 1, sl 1, k 1, p.s.s.o, k 1, (p 1, k 1) 5 times.

6th Row. (K 1, p 1) 5 times, p 4, * p 2 tog, m 1, p 1, m 1, p 2 tog, p 5. Rep from * to last 19 sts, p 2 tog, m 1, p 1, m 1, p 2 tog, p 4, (p 1, k 1) 5 times.

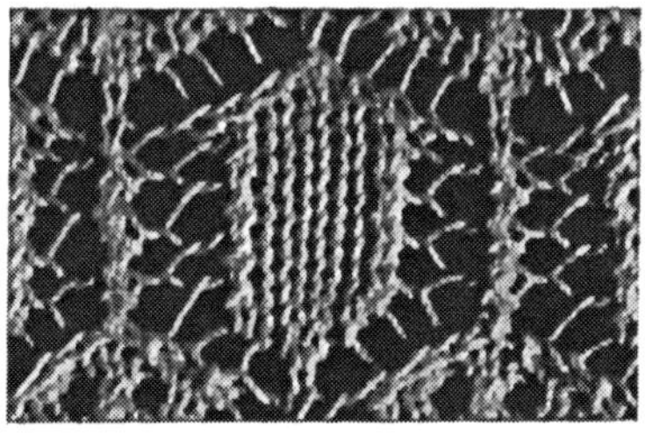

7th Row. (K 1, p 1) 5 times, k 3, * k 2 tog, m 1, k 3, m 1, sl 1, k 1, p.s.s.o, k 3. Rep from * to last 10 sts, (p 1, k 1) 5 times.
8th Row. (K 1, p 1) 5 times, p 2, * p 2 tog, m 1, p 5, m 1, p 2 tog, p 1. Rep from * to last 11 sts, p 1, (p 1, k 1) 5 times.
9th Row. (K 1, p 1) 5 times, k 1, k 2 tog, m 1, * k 7, m 1, sl 1, k 2 tog, p.s.s.o, m 1. Rep from * to last 20 sts, k 7, m 1, k 2 tog, k 1, (p 1, k 1) 5 times.
10th Row. (K 1, p 1) 5 times, * p 3, m 1, p 2 tog, p 3, p 2 tog, m 1. Rep from * to last 13 sts, p 3, (p 1, k 1) 5 times.
11th to 16th Row. Rep 9th and 10th rows 3 times more.
These 16 rows form the patt. Rep them 13 times more, then rep rows 1 to 8 inclusive once.
Work 10 rows in m st. Cast off in m st.
Starch the cloth, pin out and leave to dry. Make a knotted fringe at each end.

Knitted Tray Cloth

Materials. Mercer-Crochet No. 20 (20 gram). 3 balls selected colour. 5 Milwards' Double-pointed Knitting Needles No. 14.

Tension. 9 sts=1 in. measured over pattern.

Measurements. $12\frac{1}{2}$ in. $\times$ $17\frac{1}{2}$ in.

Cast on 61 sts on 1st needle, 1 st on 2nd needle, 61 sts on 3rd needle, 1 st on 4th needle.
Using 5th needle work thus:
1st Round. *1st needle:* K into front and back of 1st st, k to last 2 sts, k into front and back of next st, k 1. *2nd needle:* K 3 times into st (front, back, front again). *3rd and 4th needles:* As 1st and 2nd needles.

2nd Round. Knit.
3rd Round. *1st needle:* Inc in 1st st, k to last 2 sts, inc in next st, k 1. *2nd needle:* Inc in 1st and 2nd sts, k 1. *3rd and 4th needles:* As 1st and 2nd needles.
4th Round. Knit.
5th Round. *1 st needle:* Inc in 1st st, k to last 2 sts, inc in next st, k 1. *2nd, 3rd and 4th needles:* As 1st needle.
6th Round. Knit.
Rep last 2 rounds 9 times.
25th Round. *1st needle:* P twice into 1st st, p to last 2 sts, p twice into next st, p 1. *2nd, 3rd and 4th needles:* As 1st needle.
26th Round. Knit.
27th Round. *1st needle:* * K 6, k 2 tog. Rep from * to last 7 sts, k 7. *2nd needle:* Knit. *3rd and 4th needles:* As 1st and 2nd needles. (77-27-77-27.)
28th Round. *1st needle:* Inc in 1st st, k 3, * k 4, m 1, k 2 tog, k 4. Rep from * to last 3 sts, k 1, inc in next st, k 1. *2nd, 3rd and 4th needles;* As 1st needle.
29th Round. *1st needle:* P 5, * p 4, k 2, p 4. Rep from * to last 4 sts, p 4. *2nd, 3rd and 4th needles:* As 1st needle.
30th Round. *1st needle:* Inc in 1st st, k 4, * k 3, m 1, k 2 tog, m 1, k 2 tog, k 3. Rep from * to last 4 sts, k 2, inc in next st, k 1. *2nd, 3rd and 4th needles:* As 1st needle.
31st Round. *1st needle:* P 6, * p 3, k 4, p 3. Rep from * to last 5 sts, p 5. *2nd, 3rd and 4th needles:* As 1st needle.
32nd Round. *1st needle:* Inc in 1st st, k 5, * k 2, (m 1, k 2 tog) 3 times, k 2. Rep from * to last 5 sts, k 3, inc in next st, k 1. *2nd, 3rd and 4th needles:* As 1st needle.
33rd Round. *1st needle:* P 7, * p 2, k 6, p 2. Rep from * to last 6 sts, p 6. *2nd, 3rd and 4th needles:* As 1st needle.
34th Round. *1st needle:* Inc in 1st st, k 6, * k 1, (m 1, k 2 tog) 4 times, k 1. Rep from * to last 6 sts, k 4, inc in next st, k 1. *2nd, 3rd and 4th needles:* As 1st needle.
35th Round. *1st needle:* P 8, * p 1, k 8, p 1. Rep from * to last 7 sts, p 7. *2nd, 3rd and 4th needles:* As 1st needle.
36th Round. *1st needle:* Inc in 1st st, k 7, * m 1, k 2 tog. Rep from * to last 7 sts, k 5, inc in next st, k 1. *2nd, 3rd and 4th needles:* As 1st needle.
37th Round. *1st needle:* P 9, k to last 8 sts, p 8. *2nd, 3rd and 4th needles:* As 1st needle.
38th Round. *1st needle:* Inc in 1st st, k 8, * k 1, (m 1, k 2 tog) 4 times, k 1. Rep from * to last 8 sts, k 6, k twice into next st, k 1. *2nd, 3rd and 4th needles:* As 1st needle.
39th Round. *1st needle:* P 10, * p 1, k 8, p 1. Rep from * to last 9 sts, p 9. *2nd, 3rd and 4th needles:* As 1st needle.
40th Round. *1st needle:* Inc in 1st st, k 9, * k 2, (m 1, k 2 tog) 3 times, k 2. Rep from * to last 9 sts, k 7, k twice into next st, k 1. *2nd, 3rd and 4th needles:* As 1st needle.
41st Round. *1st needle:* P 11, * p 2, k 6, p 2. Rep from * to last 10 sts, p 10. *2nd, 3rd and 4th needles:* As 1st needle.
42nd Round. *1st needle:* Inc in 1st st, k 10, * k 3, (m 1, k 2 tog) twice, k 3. Rep from * to last 10 sts, k 8, k twice into next st, k 1. *2nd, 3rd and 4th needles:* As 1st needle.

(continued on page 112)

Knitted Lace Edgings

Materials. Mercer-Crochet No. 15 (20 gram). 3 balls white or ecru. 1 pair Milwards' Phantom Knitting Pins No. 14.

Measurements. Nos. 1, 2 and 3= 1 in. wide. No. 4=1½ in. deep.

Edging No. 1

Cast on 9 sts.

1st Row. Sl 2, k 2, m 1, k 2 tog from back (ktb), m 3, ktb, k 1.

2nd Row. M 1, ktb, k 1, p 1, k 3, m 1, ktb, p 2.

3rd Row. Sl 2, k 2, m 1, ktb, k 5.

4th Row. M 1, ktb, k 5, m 1, ktb, p 2.

5th and 6th Rows. As 3rd and 4th rows.

7th Row. Sl 2, k 2, m 1, ktb, k 2, m 3, ktb, k 1.

8th Row. M 1, ktb, k 1, p 1, k 5, m 1, ktb, p 2.

9th Row. Sl 2, k 2, m 1, ktb, p 2, k 5.

10th Row. K 9, m 1, ktb, p 2.

11th Row. Sl 2, k 2, m 1, ktb, m 3, ktb. The 5 sts remaining are to be cast off as follows: Sl 3 on to right-hand pin, pass the 5th st over the 4th st, pass the 3rd st back on to left-hand pin and slip 4th st over it, pass the 2nd st back on to left-hand pin and slip the 3rd st over it, pass the 1st st back on to left-hand pin and slip the 2nd st over it. Knit the remaining st. Repeat 2nd to 11th row inclusive for length required.

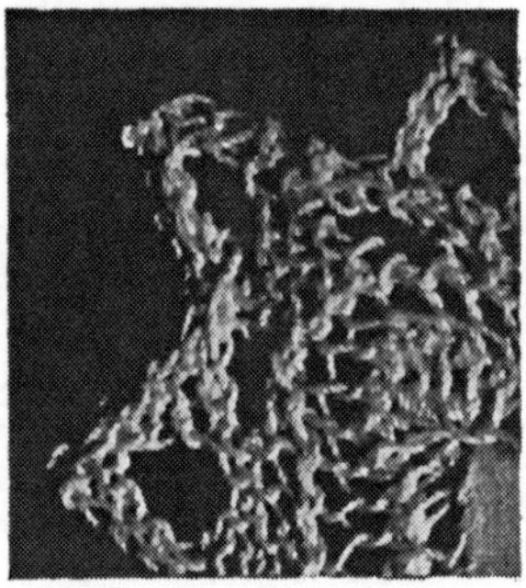

Edging No. 2

Cast on 8 sts.

1st Row. Sl 1, k 2, m 1, p 2 tog, m 2, p 2 tog, k 1 at back.

2nd Row. Sl 1, k 2, p 1, k 2, m 1, p 2 tog, k 1 at back.

3rd Row. Sl 1, k 2, m 1, p 2 tog, k 1, m 2, p 2 tog, k 1 at back.

4th Row. Sl 1, k 2, p 1, k 3, m 1, p 2 tog, k 1 at back.

5th Row. Sl 1, k 2, m 1, p 2 tog, k 2, m 2, p 2 tog, k 1 at back.

6th Row. Sl 1, k 2, p 1, k 4, m 1, p 2 tog, k 1 at back.

7th Row. Sl 1, k 2, m 1, p 2 tog, k 5, k 1 at back.

8th Row. Cast off 3, k 4, m 1, p 2 tog, k 1 at back.

Repeat from 1st row for length required.

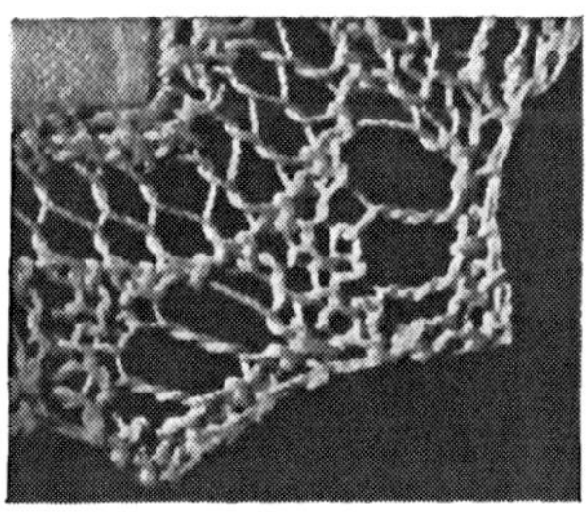

EDGING No. 2
(above)

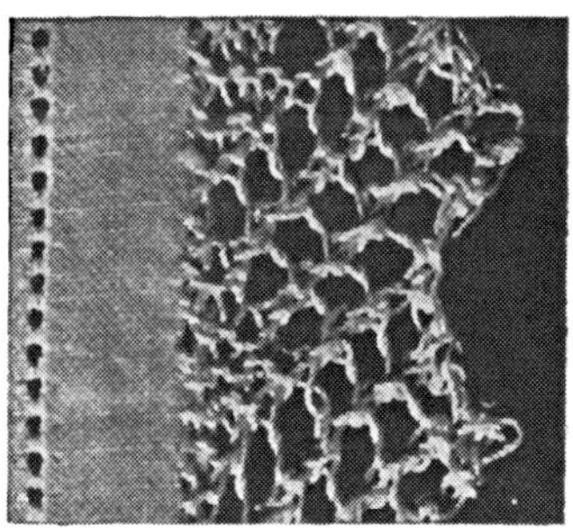

EDGING No. 3
(overleaf)

Edging No. 3

Cast on 7 sts and k one row.

Pattern (*photo on previous page*)

1st Row. K 1, (th fwd, k 2 tog) twice, th fwd, k 2.

2nd and each alternate row. M 1 by passing cotton round right-hand pin, k 2 tog, k to end.

3rd Row. K 2, (th fwd, k 2 tog) twice, th fwd, k 2.

5th Row. K 3, (th fwd, k 2 tog) twice, th fwd, k 2.

7th Row. K 4, (th fwd, k 2 tog) twice, th fwd, k 2 tog.

9th Row. K 3, (th fwd, k 2 tog) twice, th fwd, k 3 tog.

11th Row. K 2, (th fwd, k 2 tog) twice, th fwd, k 3 tog.

13th Row. K 1, (th fwd, k 2 tog) twice, th fwd, k 3 tog.

14th Row. M 1 by passing cotton round right-hand pin, k to end (8 sts).

Repeat 3rd to 14th row for length required; end with 14th row.

---

continued from page 97

14th Row. K 2 tog, k to last 2 sts, k 2 tog.

15th Row. K 2, (m 2, k 1) 14 times, k 5, * k 6, (m 2, k 1) 14 times, k 5. Repeat from * to last 21 sts, k 6, (m 2, k 1) 14 times, k 1.

16th Row. K 1, m 2, draw out the next 15 sts to long loops by dropping the make sts of the last row and p the 15 tog, (m 2, p 2 tog) twice, m 2, k 1, * k 1, (m 2, p 2 tog) twice, m 2, p 15 tog as before, (m 2, p 2 tog) twice, m 2, k 1. Repeat from * ending last repeat p 15 tog, m 2, k 1.

17th Row. (K 2, p 1) 4 times, k 1, * (k 2, p 1) 6 times, k 1. Repeat from * to last 13 sts, (k 2, p 1) 4 times, k 1.

18th to 20th Row. K.

Cast off tightly.

Shorter Edge

Cast on 120 sts and work the 20 rows of patt as for longer edge.

Edging No. 4

This edging is worked widthwise. The instructions are to fit a traycloth measuring 11½ by 15½ inches. Each pattern measures approximately 2 inches, therefore for every 2 inches extra required, add 19 sts to the number stated.

Longer Edge

Cast on 158 sts loosely.

1st to 3rd Row. K.

4th Row. K 3, * k 2, m 1, (p 3 tog, m 2) 4 times, p 3 tog, m 1, k 2. Repeat from * to last 3 sts, k 3.

5th Row. K 3, * k 5, p 1, (k 2, p 1) 3 times, k 4. Repeat from * to last 3 sts, k 3.

6th Row. K 2 tog, k to last 2 sts, k 2 tog.

7th Row. As 6th row.

8th Row. K 2 tog, m 2, p 2 tog, k 13, p 2 tog, m 2, k 1, * k 1, m 2, p 2 tog, k 13, p 2 tog, m 2, k 1. Repeat from * to last 20 sts, k 1, m 2, p 2 tog, k 13, p 2 tog, m 2, k 2 tog.

G

9th Row. * K 2, p 1, k 15, p 1, k 2. Repeat from * to end.

10th Row. K 2 tog, k to last 2 sts, k 2 tog.

11th Row. As 10th row.

12th Row. K 1, m 2, p 2 tog, k 11, (p 2 tog, m 2) twice, k 1, * k 1, (m 2, p 2 tog) twice, k 11, (p 2 tog, m 2) twice, k 1. Repeat from * to last 19 sts, k 1, (m 2, p 2 tog) twice, k 11, p 2 tog, m 2, k 1.

13th Row. K 2, p 1, k 13, (p 1, k 2) twice, * (k 2, p 1) twice, k 13, (p 1, k 2) twice. Repeat from * to last 22 sts, (k 2, p 1) twice, k 13, p 1, k 2.

continued on previous page

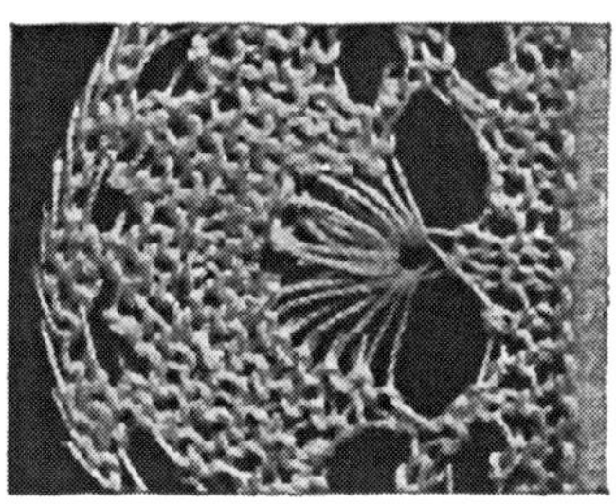

☆ NETTING ☆

VERY SIMPLE TOOLS are needed—a netting needle, gauges to form the size of the loops (ordinary knitting needles will do), and smooth, easy-running thread, such as Mercer-Crochet. The work must be anchored to a firm table to take the pull of making the stitches, or if preferred, a 'Stirrup' consisting of a piece of stout string tied into a loop long enough to go under the foot and round the knee, can be used instead. In both cases a loop of the working thread is the basis on which the work is done, (see diagram No. 89).

First wind the thread round the needle, taking care that no more thread is wound than the size of the woven mesh allows. Then tie the end of the thread to the working loop. Holding the gauge between the thumb and first finger of the left hand and working over the three middle fingers, pass the thread round from front to back then to the left under the thumb, then to the right over and behind the gauge to the front of the work (see diagram No. 90). Now pass the needle through the loop over the fingers and also the loop of the previous row (or the working loop when working the first row) (see diagram No. 91), then pull up the knot, guiding it with the little finger (see diagram No. 92).

The work is always done from left to right and, therefore, is turned at the end of each row.

Fig. 89

1. Working or Foundation Loop

The thread is shown tied to the loop and two stitches or knots have been made (Fig. 89).

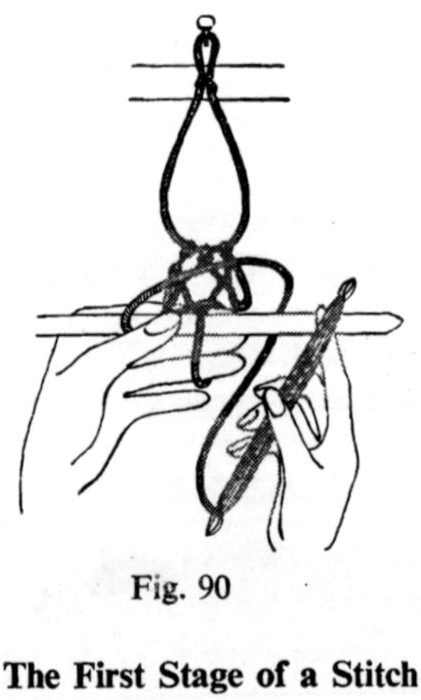

Fig. 90

2. The First Stage of a Stitch

The thread is passed round the three middle fingers of the left hand and kept in place by the thumb (Fig. 90).

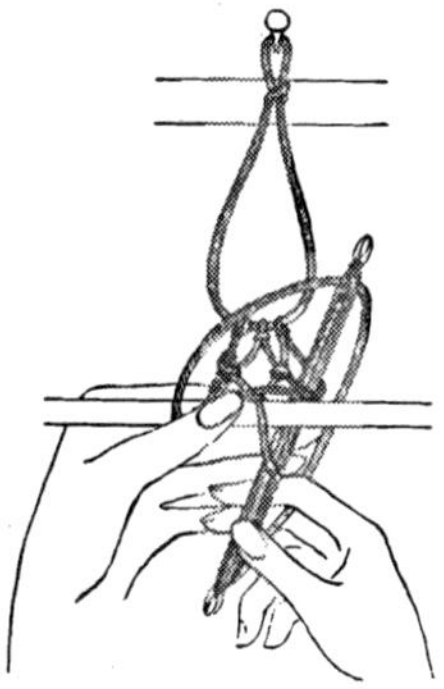

Fig. 91

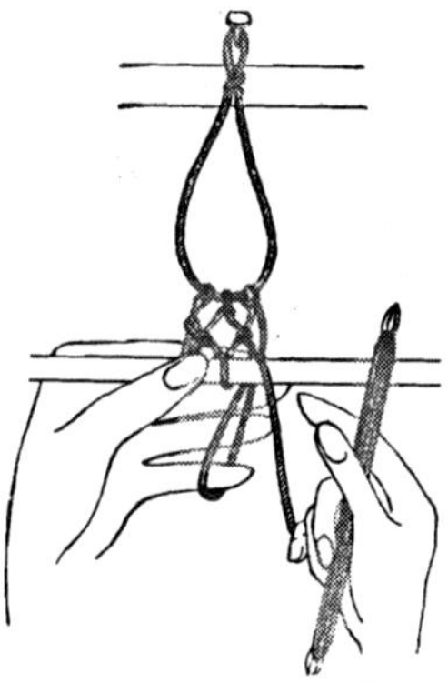

Fig. 92

3. The Second Stage of a Stitch

The needle is inserted through the loop round the fingers and into the loop of the previous row (Fig. 91).

4. The Third Stage of a Stitch

The loop is about to be pulled into position, guided by the little finger (Fig. 92).

Netted Fichu

(See photograph overleaf)

Materials. Mercer-Crochet No. 20 (20 gram). 2 balls selected colour. 1 Netting Needle. 1 Milwards' Phantom Knitting Pin No. 6 and No. 3 for gauge. 1 Milwards' Steel Crochet Hook No. 3.

Measurements. $23\frac{1}{2} \times 47$ in.

Begin with the triangular centre using the No. 6 pin and work as explained in diagram 89, withdraw the gauge, turn the work and proceed as shown in the following three diagrams, increasing a stitch in every row by working two stitches into the last loop of the previous row. When there are 77 stitches in the row, fasten off securely. Take the work off the working loop and draw up the loops with the tied end. Fasten off. To make the frill which is worked along the increased edges of the triangle, pin out one edge and, using the No. 3 pin as a gauge, work two stitches into each hole until you reach the point of the triangle. Work 12 stitches into the last hole, then continue working 2 stitches into each hole along the other edge. Work 5 more rows of stitches straight and fasten off. Finish the edge by working 4 double crochet into each hole of the straight side of the triangle and 9 into each hole of the frill.

Small darned motifs can be added. These are made as shown in the diagram overleaf with an ordinary needle and 4 strands of cotton.

NETTED FICHU

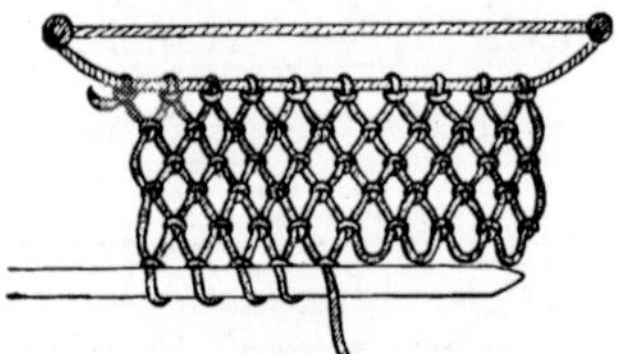

Fig. 93

This shows the method of working a straight strip of netting as used for the frill of the fichu.

Fig. 94

Method of working the darned motif on the fichu.

Long Stole with Fringed Ends

Materials. Mercer-Crochet No. 10 (20 gram). 3 balls white. 1 Milwards' Steel Netting Needle No. 17. 1 Milwards' Phantom Knitting Pin No. 6 for gauge.

Measurement. 16 in. wide × 2 yds. long.

Begin at one corner as shown in the first diagram and increase a stitch in every row by working two stitches into the last loop of the previous row until there are 50 stitches. * Begin shaping by decreasing one stitch at the end of the next row and increasing one stitch at the end of the following row. (To increase, work twice into the same loop. To decrease, take two loops together.)

Continue increasing and decreasing in this way until 96 rows have been worked from *. Now decrease at the end of every row until 2 stitches remain. Fasten off.

Pin out the scarf to form a perfect rectangle, damp well and press. The fringe is made by knotting 6 strands of cotton 3 in. long into each hole.

☆HAIRPIN LACE CROCHET☆

THIS PARTICULARLY charming type of crochet has a wide variety of uses; such as edging for collars, handkerchiefs, tray-mats and guest towels, etc., and to form an all-over fabric for blouses, dickies, collars, etc.

Hairpin crochet is very easy to do and uses a comparatively small amount of material as long loops form the largest part of the fabric. All sizes of Mercer-Crochet cotton can be used, the selected size depending upon the type of article to be trimmed and whether the edging or fabric is to be coarse or fine.

Experiment with odd lengths of Mercer-Crochet, No. 5 or 10, and a prong 1¼ in. across until the desired effect is obtained.

HOW TO WORK THE LACE

Use a crochet hook and a Hairpin Lace staple. Hold the crochet hook in the right hand. Make a loop at end of ball thread and slip on to crochet hook. Take the hairpin in the left hand and hold it flat between the thumb and first finger, with prong end uppermost and the round part downwards in the palm of the hand (see Steps 1 to 7).

STEP 1. Make a loop at end of ball thread (Fig. 95).

STEP 2. Insert hook in loop and wind ball thread around right prong of Hairpin (Fig. 95).

STEP 3. Thread over hook and draw through loop, keeping loop at centre (Fig. 95).

STEP 4. Raise hook to a vertical position and turn Hairpin to the left (Fig. 96).

STEP 5. Thread over hook and draw through loop on hook (Fig. 97).

STEP 6. Insert hook into loop of left prong (Fig. 98).

STEP 7. Thread over hook and draw loop through (2 loops on hook), thread over and draw through remaining 2 loops.

Repeat Steps 4 to 7 until Hairpin is filled.

Remove all loops, re-insert Hairpin into last 4 loops and continue as before for length required.

Fig. 95

Fig. 96

Fig. 97

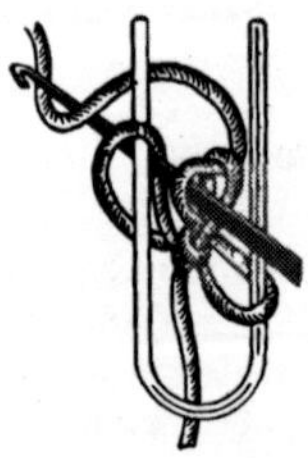

Fig. 98

Handkerchief Edging

Materials. Mercer-Crochet No. 40 (20 gram). 1 ball selected colour. 1 Handkerchief. Milwards' Steel Crochet Hook No. 4. Hairpin Staple $1\frac{1}{4}$ in. wide (No. 1 Minerva).

Work a strip long enough to go all round handkerchief without stretching and allowing an extra inch to turn each corner.
Work the following crochet edging along the side which is to be sewn to the handkerchief:
Make a loop on the hook, insert hook from back into each of the following 6 loops of the strip, thread over and draw through 6 loops, thread over and draw through remaining 2 loops on hook (a cluster made), * 6 ch, 1 cluster over next 6 loops; repeat from * until there is sufficient to go along one side of handkerchief.

Work corners as follows:

Insert hook from back into each of the following 12 loops and complete a cluster as before. Make another 6-loop cluster and repeat from * for other 3 sides, ending with a 12-loop cluster, 1 ss into top of first cluster. Fasten off.

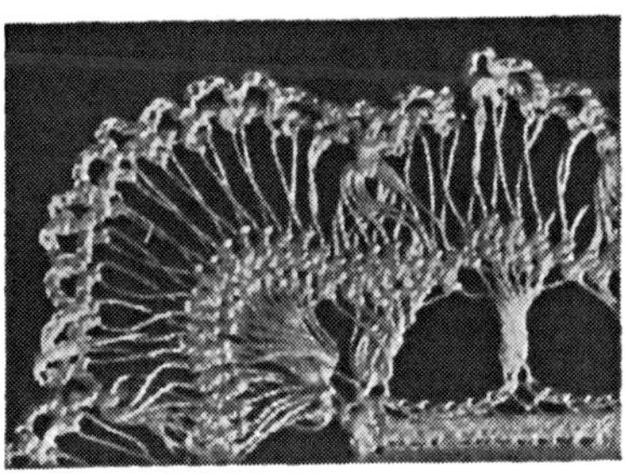

OUTER EDGE

1st Row. * Work a cluster over a cluster on the inner edge, (2 ch, 1 dc into next loop—from back) 6 times, 2 ch; repeat from * to corner. At corners work a 6-loop cluster over last 6-loop clusters at inner edge, (2 ch, 1 dc into next loop) 12 times, 2 ch; repeat from first * all round outer edge, ending with 1 ss into top of first cluster.

2nd Row. Ss to first dc, 1 dc into same place as last ss, * 4 ch, 1 dc into next dc; repeat from * 4 times more, 4 ch, miss dc of cluster, 1 dc into next dc; repeat from * all round, working 4 ch and 1 dc into each dc at corners, ending with 1 ss into first dc. Fasten off.

Hairpin Lace Dickie

Materials. Mercer-Crochet No. 40 (20 gram). 3 balls selected colour. 1 Hairpin Staple 1¼ in. wide (No. 1 Minerva). Milwards' Steel Crochet Hook No. 4. Net Back. Small piece Cotton Wool. 1 yd. Narrow Ribbon.

Measurements. Length from shoulder to bottom edge=19 in. Width across front=12½ in.

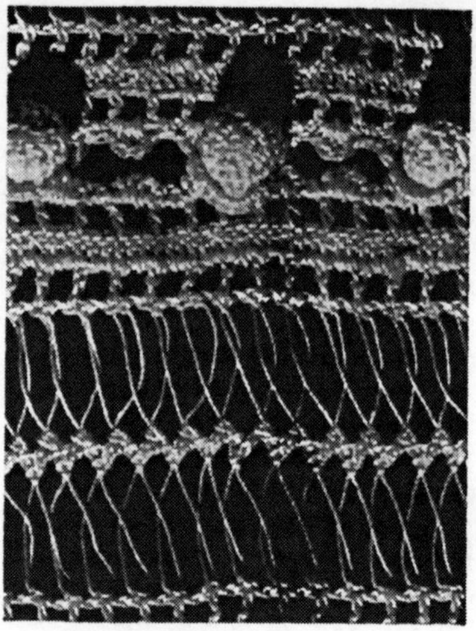

FIRST STRIP

Make a strip of Hairpin Lace working steps 4 to 7 until there are 117 loops on each prong of staple and working 3 dc into loop instead of one dc. This makes a more elaborate centre to the strip which is very effective.

Crochet Edging

1st Row. Join thread in first loop at one side of Hairpin Lace (keeping loop twisted), 1 dc into same place as join, * 1 ch, 1 dc into next (twisted) loop; repeat from * to end of loops, 5 ch, turn.

2nd Row. Miss first dc, 1 tr into next dc, * 2 ch, 1 tr into next dc; repeat from * to end of row (116 sps), 1 ch, turn.

3rd Row. 1 dc 3 tr and 1 dc into first sp (shell made), 1 dc into next sp, * 1 dc 3 tr and 1 dc into next sp, 1 dc into next sp; repeat from * to end of row. Fasten off.

Join thread in first loop on opposite side of Hairpin Lace and work same as 1st and 2nd rows of other side of crochet edging, turning with 3 ch at end of 2nd row.

3rd Row. * 2 tr into next sp, 1 tr into next tr; repeat from * ending with 2 tr into last sp, 1 tr into 3rd of 5 turning ch, 5 ch, turn.

4th Row. Miss first 3 tr, 1 tr into next tr, * 2 ch, miss 2 tr, 1 tr into next tr; repeat from * ending with 2 ch, miss 2 tr, 1 tr into top of turning ch. Fasten off. (This is outside edge.)

SECOND STRIP

Make another strip of Hairpin Lace with 117 loops on each prong. Fasten off.

Crochet Edging

Work 1st and 2nd rows same as previous edging.

3rd Row. Work as for 3rd row of edging until 49 shells in all have been worked. Fasten off.

On opposite side of loops work 1st and 2nd rows as before.

3rd Row. 1 dc and 2 tr into first sp, 1 ss into centre tr of corresponding

shell of First Strip, 1 tr and 1 dc into same sp on second strip, * 1 dc into next sp on second strip, 1 dc and 2 tr into next sp, 1 ss into centre tr of next shell of first strip, 1 tr and 1 dc into same sp on second strip; repeat from * to end of row. Fasten off.

THIRD STRIP

Make another strip of Hairpin Lace with 99 loops on each prong. Fasten off.

Crochet Edging

Work same as 1st and 2nd rows of edging having 98 sps instead of 116 sps.

3rd Row. As 3rd row (joining row) of second strip.

Along other side work 1st to 4th row as in first strip then 1 shell row. Fasten off. (This finishes one half.)

Make another half front exactly the same but join the last shell row to the first half for 9 in. up from lower edge, leaving remaining part open. Continue working shells along the open edge of sps, then work round neck as follows: 3 dc over side of tr, 3 dc over next sp, 9 ch, 1 dc into dc at centre of Hairpin Lace, 9 ch, 3 dc over next sp, 1 dc into end of shell, 2 ch, 1 ss into tr of first free sp at neck, ss along to end of next sp, 3 ch, turn. Work 12 sps back to front open edge, 2 ch, turn.

Next Row. (1 dc into next sp, 1 dc into next tr) 6 times, 1 hlf tr into next sp, 1 hlf tr into next tr, 1 tr into next sp, 1 tr into next tr, 1 dbl tr into next sp, 1 dbl tr into next tr, 1 trip tr into next sp, 1 trip tr into next tr, miss next sp and also next free sp at neck, 1 trip tr into next tr, 1 trip tr into next sp, 1 trip tr into next tr, 1 dbl tr into next sp, 1 tr into next tr, 1 tr into next sp, 1 hlf tr into next tr, 1 hlf tr into next sp, * 1 dc into next tr, 1 dc into next sp; repeat from * to top. Fasten off. This edging should turn the square shaping at neck into a round.

Join thread to the opposite opening and work to correspond but do not fasten off.

Work across shoulder: 2 ch, 3 dc into sp, 9 ch, 1 dc into dc at centre of Hairpin Lace, 9 ch, 3 dc over next sp, 3 ch, 1 dc between shells, 3 ch, 3 dc over next sp, 9 ch, 1 dc into dc at centre of Hairpin Lace, 9 ch, 3 dc over sp, 3 dc over tr of row-end, 3 dc over next sp, 5 ch, turn.

Work 23 sps back to neck end, 3 ch, turn. (2 tr into next sp, 1 tr into next tr) 23 times, 3 ch, 2 tr over tr just made, 2 tr into next sp, 1 tr into next dc, now work 2 tr into next sp, 1 tr into next tr to bottom edge. Fasten off.

Work other shoulder and side tr to correspond, then work 68 sps along lower edge, then 1 row of tr, 1 row of sp and 1 row of tr. Fasten off.

BOW TIE

1st Row. Commence with 4 ch, 1 dc into 3rd ch from hook, 2 ch, turn.

2nd Row. 1 dc into dc, 1 dc into turning ch, 2 ch, turn.

3rd Row. 1 dc into each dc, 2 dc into turning ch, 2 ch, turn.

Repeat 3rd row until there are 10 dc in all.

Now continue working on these 10 dc until strip measures 30 in. long, then decrease one st on each row until one st only remains. Fasten off. (To decrease—insert hook into st and pull thread through, insert hook into next st and pull thread through, thread over and pull through all loops on hook.)

BUTTONS

Commence with 6 ch, join with a ss to form a ring.

1st Row. Into ring work 12 dc.

Continue working 1 dc into each dc to form a tiny cap. Stuff with cotton wool and draw up opening. Fasten off. Make seven buttons.

TO MAKE UP

Press with a hot iron. Sew on net back to crochet shoulders, then carefully sew on collar, leaving sufficient to make into a bow at each end. Work 7 loops down right front opening and sew on buttons to correspond. Cut ribbon into 4 lengths and sew on to back and front at side edges.

☆ BRAIDWORK ☆

A HEAVY TYPE of lace can be made with this form of braidwork. It is simple to construct and can be worked successfully in Mercer-Crochet cotton of all sizes. A sufficiently long length of braid is made first. The design is transferred or traced on to a piece of stiff muslin. The braid is then applied to the design and tacked in position. The button-hole bars are then made (note that the stitches do not enter the muslin). When the braid is held firmly in position with the required number of button-hole bars, the tacking stitches are removed and the braidwork is freed from the muslin and is complete.

Fig. 99.

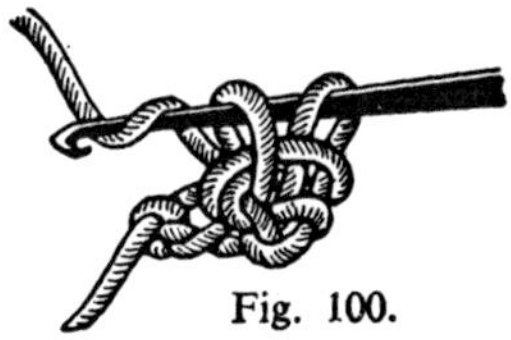

Fig. 100.

Fig. 101.

METHOD OF WORKING BRAID

Commence with 2 ch, then holding this between the finger and thumb of the left hand, work 1 double crochet into the first chain made (Fig. 99), turn, 1 dc into foundation loop of 2nd ch made, inserting hook into back of loop (Fig. 100), * turn, insert hook into 2 loops at side (Fig. 101), thread over and draw through 2 loops, thread over and draw through remaining 2 loops; repeat from * for length required. Fasten off.

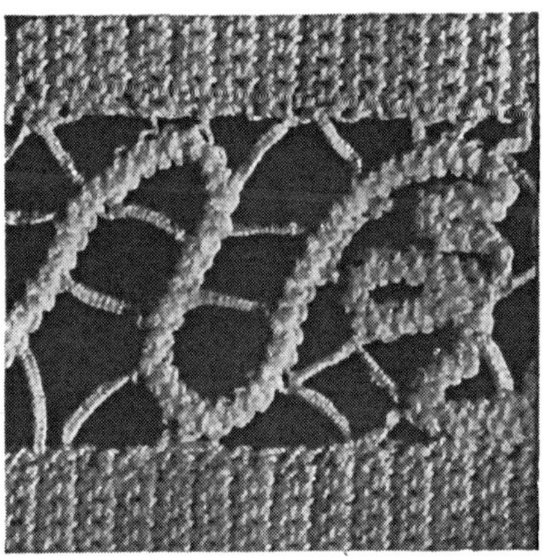

Detail of Braidwork on Place Mat—overleaf.

Braid Trimmed Place Mat

Materials. Mercer-Crochet No. 20 (20 gram). 1 ball selected colour. Milwards' Steel Crochet Hook No. 3. Piece of Linen 7½ in. × 10½ in.

Work braid as given above and tack in position on the foundation (Fig. 103). Work strips of dc to outline the lace as follows:

Commence with 10 ch.

1st Row. 1 dc into 2nd ch from hook, 1 dc into each ch, 2 ch, turn.

2nd Row. Miss first dc, 1 dc into each dc, 2 ch, turn. Repeat 2nd row until strip is long enough to fit braid piece. Make other 3 pieces in same manner. Sew one on each side of braid and then work buttonhole bars as shown on Fig. 102.

Lay a small hem all round linen and work a row of dc all round.

Overcast lace to each end of linen.

EDGING

1st Row. Join thread and work a row of dc all round mat working 3 dc into same place at corners, join with a ss into first dc.

2nd and 3rd Rows. 1 dc into each dc, work 3 dc into centre dc at corners, join with 1 ss into first dc. Fasten off.

Fig. 102.

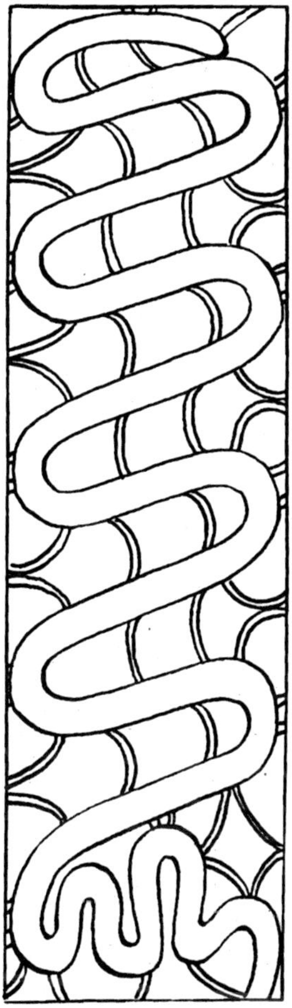

CENTRE

Fig. 103.

Three Useful Fringes

IN KNITTING, HAIRPIN-WORK AND CROCHET

Depth of Fringe=3 in.

1. CROCHET EDGING WITH

Tassel Fringe

Use either No. 5 or 10 Mercer-Crochet and Milwards' Steel Crochet Hook No. 2½. Work the crochet strip to fit the object to which it is to be sewn as follows:

Commence with 22 ch.

1st Row. 1 tr into 7th ch from hook, 1 tr into next ch, 2 ch, miss 2 ch, 1 dc into next ch, 5 ch, miss 3 ch, 1 dc into next ch, 3 ch, miss 2 ch, 1 tr into each of next 2 ch, 2 ch, miss 2 ch, 1 tr into last ch, 5 ch, turn.

2nd Row. Miss first tr, 1 tr into each of next 2 tr, 3 ch, 1 dc into next 5 ch loop, 3 ch, 1 tr into each of next 2 tr, 2 ch, 1 tr into 3rd of turning ch, 5 ch, turn.

3rd Row. Miss first tr, 1 tr into each

of next 2 tr, 2 ch, 1 dc into next loop, 3 tr into next dc, 1 dc into next loop, 2 ch, 1 tr into each of next 2 tr, 2 ch, 1 tr into 3rd of turning ch, 5 ch, turn.
4th Row. Miss first tr, 1 tr into each of next 2 tr, 5 ch, 1 dc into 2nd of next 3 tr, 5 ch, 1 tr into each of next 2 tr, 2 ch, 1 tr into 3rd of turning ch, 5 ch, turn.
5th Row. Miss first tr, 1 tr into each of next 2 tr, 2 ch, 1 dc into next loop, 4 ch, 1 dc into next loop, 2 ch, 1 tr into each of next 2 tr, 2 ch, 1 tr into 3rd of turning ch, 5 ch, turn.
6th Row. Miss first tr, 1 tr into each of next 2 tr, 9 ch, 1 tr into each of next 2 tr, 2 ch, 1 tr into 3rd of turning ch, 5 ch, turn.
7th Row. Miss first tr, 1 tr into each of next 2 tr, 2 ch, 1 dc into next loop, 5 ch, 1 dc into same loop, 2 ch, 1 tr into each of next 2 tr, 2 ch, 1 tr into 3rd of turning ch, 5 ch, turn.
Repeat 2nd to 7th row for length required, omitting turning ch on last row.

EDGING
Work along top edge of strip as follows: 2 dc into each sp and 1 dc into top or bottom of each tr. Fasten off. Work along lower edge in same manner, 1 ch, turn. Now work a picot edge thus: 1 dc into each of first 3 dc, * 3 ch, 1 ss into last dc, 1 dc into each of next 4 dc, miss 1 dc, 1 dc into each of next 4 dc, 3 ch, 1 ss into last dc, 1 dc into each of next 8 dc; repeat from * to end. Fasten off. Make the tassels as shown in diagram and sew on to *missed* dc on edging, thus leaving 2 picot loops between each tassel.

TASSEL
1. Wind the thread 80 times over a piece of stout card $1\frac{1}{2}$ in. wide. Thread a loop through the threads at one edge of the card. This can be a chain loop or a number of threads as preferred.
2. Take off from the card and bind firmly. Cut and trim the ends.

TASSEL

2. Knitted Fringe

Use Mercer-Crochet of a suitable thickness in relation to the article to be trimmed. For a fairly thick fringe suitable for trimming lamp shades, curtains, etc., use 4 thicknesses of

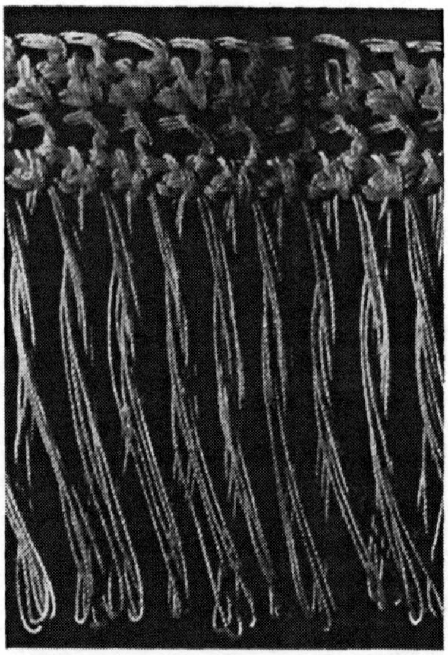

Depth of Fringe = $3\frac{1}{2}$ in.

No. 5 cotton from 4 separate balls and a pair of short No. 10 needles. Cast on 9 stitches (all rows are the same), * m 1 (by passing all four strands of cotton round the needle), k 2 tog, k 1. Repeat from * twice more. Work for the required length, cast off 6 stitches and fasten these off. Slip remaining 2 stitches off needle and unravel back to beginning of the work.

3. *Hairpin-Work Fringe*

No. 5 or 10 Mercer-Crochet is best for this work. Use a No. $2\frac{1}{2}$ crochet hook and a No. 1 Minerva Hairpin. Make a strip of hairpin work the required length and then edge it as follows: Work a dc into the first two loops together (putting the hook through from front to back), * 3 ch, 1 dc into next two loops in the same way. Repeat from * to end of the strip and then work the other edge in the same way.

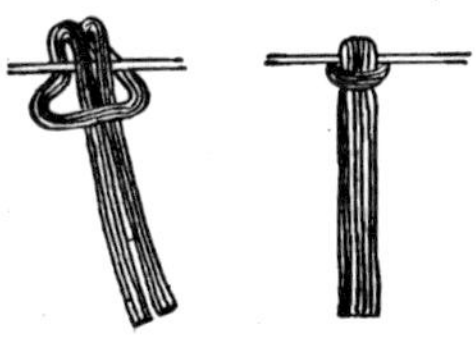

1. This shows exactly how the threads are doubled and passed through the loop to make a knot.

2. The threads are pulled up tight.

3. The knotted fringe is knotted again alternating the ends.

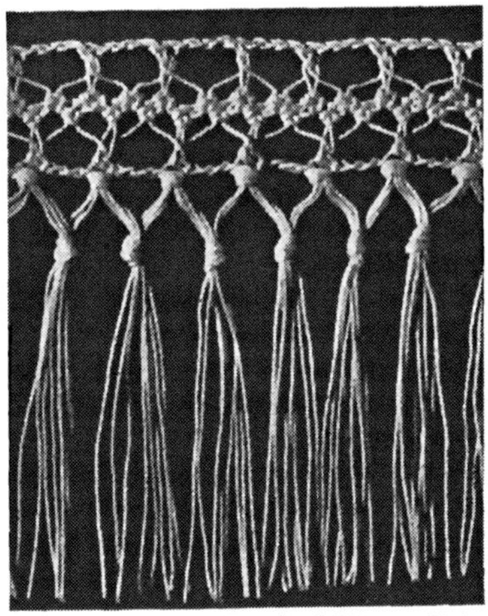

Depth of Fringe=$3\frac{1}{8}$ in.

Now add the fringe. Wind the thread eight times round a piece of card the width you want the fringe to be, plus $\frac{1}{2}$ inch for the knot. Cut so that you have 4 strands of thread and make the fringe as shown in diagrams. A crochet hook should be used for pulling the ends through the loop made in the hairpin work strip.

Tassel

WITH COVERED TOP

Wind the thread 100 times over a stout card 4 in. wide. Secure at the top with a 10 ch loop. Take off the card and bind tightly as shown in diagram overleaf.

TASSEL * page 112

Make a crochet top as follows:
Commence with 4 ch, join with a ss to form a ring.
1st Row. * 1 dc into ring, 1 ch; repeat from * twice more.
2nd Row. * 1 dc into next dc, 1 ch, 1 dc into next ch, 1 ch; repeat from * to end of row.
3rd Row. * 1 dc into next dc, 1 ch; repeat from * to end of row.
Repeat 3rd row 4 times more, ending with 1 ss into first dc. Fasten off leaving an end.
Pull the 10 ch loop of tassel through the cap which should fit neatly over the double end. Stitch the lower edge to the tassel using the left-over thread. Fasten off.

Length of Tassel=3⅜ in.

Continued from page 93

43rd Round. *1st needle:* P 12, * p 3, k 4, p 3. Rep from * to last 11 sts, p 11. *2nd, 3rd and 4th needles:* As 1st needle.
44th Round. *1st needle:* Inc in 1st st, k 11, * k 4, m 1, k 2 tog, k 4. Rep from * to last 11 sts, k 9, inc in next st, k 1. *2nd, 3rd and 4th needles:* As 1st needle.
45th Round. *1st needle:* P 13, * p 4, k 2, p 4. Rep from * to last 12 sts, p 12. *2nd, 3rd and 4th needles:* As 1st needle.
46th Round. *1st needle:* K twice into 1st st, k to last 2 sts, k twice into next st, k 1. *2nd, 3rd and 4th needles:* As 1st needle.
47th Round. Knit.
48th Round. Purl.
49th Round. As 46th round.
50th Round. *1st needle:* Inc in 1st st, * m 1, k 2 tog. Rep from * to last 2 sts, inc in next st, k 1. *2nd, 3rd and 4th needles:* As 1st needle.
51st Round. *1st needle:* K 2, * k 2 tog, m 1. Rep from * to last 3 sts, k 3. *2nd, 3rd and 4th needles:* As 1st needle.
52nd Round. *1st needle:* Inc in 1st st, k 1, * m 1, k 2 tog. Rep from * to last 3 sts, k 1, inc in next st, k 1. *2nd, 3rd and 4th needles:* As 1st needle.
53rd Round. *1st needle:* K 3, * k 2 tog, m 1. Rep from * to last 4 sts, k 4. *2nd, 3rd and 4th needles:* As 1st needle.
54th to 63rd Round. Rep rounds 50 to 53 inclusive twice, then the 50th and 51st rounds again.
64th to 67th Round. Rep 46th, 48th and 49th rounds once, then 47th round.
Now rep rounds 28 to 66 inclusive once more.
To complete border rep 48th and 49th rounds twice, then the 48th round again.
Cast off fairly loosely.
Join centre seam neatly. Starch and pin out into shape.

Lightning Source UK Ltd.
Milton Keynes UK
06 October 2010

160835UK00001B/75/P

9 781445 519586